Lawn

PROBLEM SOLVER

Meredith® Books
Des Moines, Iowa

Ortho Lawn Problem Solver

Editor: Denny Schrock
Contributing Editor: Kate Carter Frederick
Contributing Technical Editor: Michael D. Smith
Contributing Writer: Lynn Steiner
Copy Chief: Terri Fredrickson
Publishing Operations Manager: Karen Schirm
Senior Editor, Asset and Information Manager:
  Phillip Morgan
Edit and Design Production Coordinator: Mary Lee Gavin
Editorial and Design Assistant: Kathleen Stevens
Book Production Managers: Pam Kvitne,
  Marjorie J. Schenkelberg, Rick von Holdt, Mark Weaver
Contributing Copy Editor: Kelly Roberson
Technical Proofreader: B. Rosie Lerner
Contributing Proofreaders: Thomas E. Blackett,
  Rebecca Etchen, Jodie Littleton, Arenda Maxwell,
  Courtney Maxwell Greene, Barbara A. Rothfus,
  Wendy Pohlemus-Annibel
Contributing Map Illustrator: Jana Fothergill
Contributing Photo Researcher: Susan Ferguson
Indexer: Ellen Sherron
Other Contributors: Janet Anderson, Irene Swartz

Additional Editorial Contributions from Art Rep Services

Director: Chip Nadeau
Designer: lk Design

Meredith® Books

Executive Director, Editorial: Gregory H. Kayko
Executive Director, Design: Matt Strelecki
Managing Editor: Amy Tincher-Durik
Executive Editor/Group Manager: Benjamin W. Allen
Senior Associate Design Director: Tom Wegner
Marketing Product Manager: Brent Wiersma

Publisher and Editor in Chief: James D. Blume
Editorial Director: Linda Raglan Cunningham
Executive Director, New Business Development:
  Todd M. Davis
Executive Director, Sales: Ken Zagor
Director, Operations: George A. Susral
Director, Production: Douglas M. Johnston
Director, Marketing: Amy Nichols
Business Director: Jim Leonard
Vice President and General Manager: Douglas J. Guendel

Meredith Publishing Group

President: Jack Griffin
Senior Vice President: Karla Jeffries

Meredith Corporation

Chairman of the Board: William T. Kerr
President and Chief Executive Officer: Stephen M. Lacy
In Memoriam: E.T. Meredith III (1933–2003)

Photographers

(Photographers credited may retain copyright © to the listed photographs.)
L=Left, R=Right

William Adams: 61R
Mark E. Ascerno: 35R
Ronald Calhoun: 89R
Nick Christians: 11B, 20L, 21R, 26R, 32L, 33R, 42R, 45R, 54L, 55R, 59R, 63R, 65L, 67R, 68R, 69R, 70L, 71R, 72R, 74R, 75R, 77R, 80R, 81L, 81R, 88R, 92R
Clyde L. Elmore: 73R, 82R
Tom Fermanian: 24R, 29R, 50R
D.W. Greenslade/Ardea: 37R
Richard O. Kelly: 30R
Glen Kopp: 74L
Charles Llewallen: 66R
Philip L. Nixon: 32R, 36R, 39R, 56L, 56R, 57L
David Shetlar: 58L, 58R
Curtis E. Swift: 25R
Ward Upham/Kansas State Research and Extension: 60R
Bert Wiklund/AgPix: 37L

All of us at Meredith® Books are dedicated to providing you with the information and ideas you need to enhance your home and garden. We welcome your comments and suggestions about this book. Write to us at:

Meredith Corporation
Meredith Gardening Books
1716 Locust St.
Des Moines, IA 50309–3023

If you would like to purchase any of our gardening, home improvement, cooking, crafts, or home decorating and design books, check wherever quality books are sold. Or visit us at: meredithbooks.com

If you would like more information on other Ortho products, call 800/225-2883 or visit us at: www.ortho.com

Note to the Readers: Due to differing conditions, tools, and individual skills, Meredith Corporation assumes no responsibility for any damages, injuries suffered, or losses incurred as a result of following the information published in this book. Before beginning any project, review the instructions carefully, and if any doubts or questions remain, consult local experts or authorities. Because codes and regulations vary greatly, you always should check with authorities to ensure that your project complies with all applicable local codes and regulations. Always read and observe all of the safety precautions provided by manufacturers of any tools, equipment, or supplies, and follow all accepted safety procedures.

Contents

Chapter 1
Starting Off Right

No other ground cover is as inviting for foot traffic as luxuriant turfgrass.

A healthy lawn is an important part of most home landscapes. It provides a backdrop for colorful shrubs, trees, and flowers, offers a place for children and pets to play, and provides a cool green respite for entertaining and relaxing. The keys to a healthy lawn are good soil and the right type of grass. Both of these will go a long way toward reducing insect and disease problems that can turn a nice green carpet into a lawn plagued by brown patches or thin areas.

Choosing a variety

Basically, grass is categorized as a hardy, or cool-season, variety for cold-winter areas or as a subtropical, or warm-season, variety for areas where extended freezing temperatures are rare. Whether you are installing a new lawn or caring for the lawn you already have, knowing the needs of the grass is important. If you are installing a lawn, you must choose a type that is appropriate for your climate and has maintenance requirements you can satisfy. Knowing the variety of an existing lawn helps you provide the care it needs and diagnose problems it may develop.

Other things to consider when selecting a variety of grass include the amount of sunlight available and how much use the lawn will receive. While no turfgrass will grow well in shade, some are more shade tolerant and some can stand up to foot traffic better than others.

Most lawns are a blend of grasses, which makes them more resistant to disease and insect infestation than lawns of a single type. The problems that afflict one grass may not affect another variety. The map and chart on page 5 show major climate zones and characteristics of some of the more commonly grown turfgrasses.

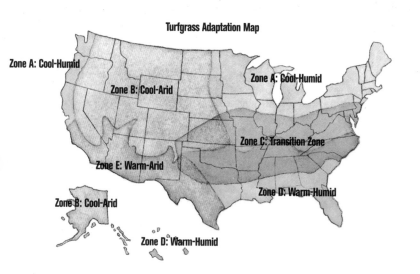

Turfgrass Adaptation Map

Zone A: Cool-Humid
Zone B: Cool-Arid
Zone A: Cool-Humid
Zone C: Transition Zone
Zone E: Warm-Arid
Zone D: Warm-Humid
Zone B: Cool-Arid
Zone D: Warm-Humid

Zones A and B- Primarily cool-season grasses. Zoysiagrass grows in the southern portions of both regions. Buffalograss grows in Zone B and drier parts of Zone A.

Zone C - This is a transition zone in which both warm-season and cool-season grasses are grown. Because warm-season grasses have long dormant periods in this zone, cool-season grasses are usually preferred. Tall fescue does particularly well in this zone.

Zones D and E - Warm-season grasses, especially bermudagrass. St. Augustinegrass, bahiagrass, and centipedegrass grow well along the Gulf Coast.

CHARACTERISTICS OF SOME GRASSES

Grass	Zone[1]	Drought Resistant	Shade Tolerant	Days to Germinate	Low Maintenance[2]
Bahiagrass	D			21–28	
Bentgrass	A		X	5–12	
Bermudagrass, common	D, E	X		14–20	X
Bermudagrass, improved	C, D, E	X		Sprigs[3]	X
Carpetgrass	D			21	
Centipedegrass	D			14–20	
Fescue, red	A, B	X	X	5–12	X
Fescue, tall	A, B, C	X	X	5–12	X
Kentucky bluegrass	A, B, C			20–30	
St. Augustinegrass	D		X	Sprigs[3]	
Zoysiagrass	C, D	X	X	Sprigs[3]	X

[1] For information on Zones, see map above.
[2] Low-maintenance turfgrasses tolerate irregular fertilizing, watering, and mowing.
[3] Usually planted as sprigs or plugs, rather than as seed.

SOIL pH AND SOIL AMENDMENTS

Before seeding or laying sod, test the soil in the lawn area to determine the pH level. The pH scale ranges from 0 to 14, with neutral at 7.0. The ideal pH for most grass is between 6.5 and 6.8. The pH affects the rate at which nutrients are released from the soil, if these nutrients are already present. Blend together soil samples from about 15 areas in the lawn, and send the mixed sample to a university or commercial soil testing service for analysis. Alternatively, you can use a home soil-testing kit, although these are not as accurate as a professional soil analysis.

Acidic soil has a pH of 5.5 or lower. Magnesium, phosphorus, and calcium are less available for plant use than in neutral soil. Nitrogen is only partially released in acidic soil because the soil organisms that free it are less active.

When soil has a pH of 5.0 or lower, soil organisms cease working altogether and no nitrogen is released.

Lawns in overly acidic soil may grow slowly. Leaves may be pale and root development may be poor. Overly acidic soil promotes disease mechanisms. Applying fertilizer may not help because the low pH stops or slows nutrient release. Neutralize acidic soil by applying finely ground dolomitic limestone, working it into the soil.

Alkaline soil has a pH above 7.0. When the pH exceeds 8.0, iron and manganese are no longer available to the grass. The lawn becomes pale or yellow. To correct alkaline soil, apply sulfur or sulfate compounds.

For a lawn to thrive, you must improve poor soil. Topsoil should be used only when you must raise the land grading. Organic

Unamended clay soil is heavy, sticky, and drains poorly.

amendments such as peat moss, compost, well-rotted manure, ground bark, and sawdust are best for improving poor soil. Adding ample organic material to clay soil can lessen the problems of runoff and compaction. Ample organic matter mixed into sandy soil helps hold moisture and nutrients in the root zone.

Soil amendments need to be applied in a layer 1–4 inches deep to effect a change in soil structure. Work the material in thoroughly with a tiller, spade, or rake.

Determine soil pH by having your soil tested.

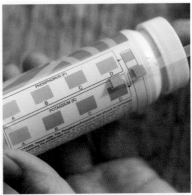

Soils with a pH below 5.5 are considered acidic; soils above 7.0 are alkaline.

INSTALLING A NEW LAWN

Use a drop spreader to evenly distribute grass seed.

Keep foot and animal traffic off a newly seeded lawn and maintain even soil moisture. Do not add nitrogen fertilizer to the lawn until seedlings have fully sprouted.

A new lawn can be installed by planting seed or laying sod. Both have advantages and disadvantages.

Seeding lawns

Successful seed sowing is a matter of seed quality, timing, effective distribution, and proper care. Always check the date on the seed container before purchasing grass seed. Buy only seed that is produced for sale in the current year.

For cool-season grasses, fall and spring planting give the best results. Fall sowing reduces the problem of heat damage to seedlings. Allow 6 weeks of growing time before the weather turns cold, usually no later than mid-September. Spring planting has the benefits of ample sunlight and rainfall. Weed growth is quite active, however, and summer heat is hard on seedlings. Most grasses do best between 50°F and 70°F. In dry weather, keep seedlings moist by covering them with a ¼- to ½-inch-deep mulch of sawdust or straw. Do not use peat moss, which promotes water runoff when dry.

Use a drop or broadcast spreader to sow seeds. Hand-distribution tends to be irregular, resulting in both bare and overly seeded areas. Rake the planted area lightly, then roll it with a light roller to ensure good seed-soil contact. Seeds should be no more than ¼ inch deep.

Sod lawns

Gardeners who do not have time to plant seed or who want an immediate lawn often prefer to lay sod. Sod comes in strips from 6–9 feet long. It should be uniformly green, moist, and ¾–1 inch thick.

Lay cool-season sod in early spring or in late summer to early fall. Lay warm-season grass sod in late spring or early summer. Prepare the soil before installation and install the sod as soon as possible after it has been cut. The sod strips should be staggered and fit snuggly against each other, but be careful not to stretch them. Keep the soil evenly moist for 2 weeks or until the sod is fully rooted.

Sodding is the best choice if you want an immediate lawn.

Chapter 2
Maintaining a Healthy Lawn

Type of Grass	Mowing Height (inches)
Bahiagrass	2–3
Bentgrass	⅜–¾
Bermudagrass	½–1½
Bluegrass	2–3
Centipedegrass	1–2
Dichondra	½–1½
Fescue, Chewings	1–2
Fescue, red	2–3
Fescue, tall	3–4
Ryegrass, annual	1½–2
Ryegrass, perennial	1–2½
St. Augustinegrass	1–2½
Zoysiagrass	½–1½

The key to a healthy lawn is maintenance. Proper mowing, watering, fertilizing, thatch control, and aeration will go a long way in reducing and preventing problems.

Mowing

In new lawns, begin to mow when the grass is 3 inches high. After the initial mowing, use the chart at right to find the height recommended for your grass variety. If your lawn is a mixture of types, cut to the length recommended for the dominant one.

Cutting a lawn too often causes grass to develop shallow roots. Shallow-rooted lawns are prone to disease and weed problems.

Mowing off too much grass at one time can lead to root decline. Eventually the lawn may develop a thin, spotty, or burned look. For best results, never remove more than one-third of the height of the grass.

Grass clippings

If you mow regularly and the clippings filter down into the turf, you can leave them on the lawn. Composting rotary mowers chop clippings small and scatter them so they do not build up into a problem. Clippings supply nitrogen as they decompose. Remove excess clippings from the lawn and add them to the compost pile or dry and use as mulch in garden beds.

Watering

A lawn needs 1–2 inches of water per week, soaking 6–8 inches deep. Clay soil has slow water penetration and needs to be watered more slowly to avoid runoff. Water moves faster through sandy soils, and they may need to be watered more often than heavy soils.

Mowing grass too short can stress a lawn, opening it up to pest problems.

Measure sprinkler output to make sure your lawn is getting the right amount of water.

FERTILIZING

Fertilizer application is dependent on many factors, including variety, climate, and level of maintenance.

Be sure to read the label and apply the appropriate amount of fertilizer for your conditions.

Evenly distribute granular fertilizers to avoid an uneven color in the lawn.

Nutrients that lawns use in large quantities are nitrogen (chemical symbol N), phosphorus (P), and potassium (K). Plants need other nutrients, but in smaller amounts, and deficiencies of these nutrients are less common.

Adequate nitrogen promotes a dark green, vigorously growing lawn. The amount required by a lawn varies with maintenance practices and the grass variety. Because nitrogen applied at excessive rates can burn grass plants and cause other problems, it is best to apply moderate amounts of fertilizer on a regular basis rather than large amounts infrequently.

The amount of potassium and phosphorus required by a lawn depends on the soil's ability to provide these nutrients. Some soils have high levels of phosphorus, making additional fertilizer unnecessary. The only way to determine the amount is to have your soil tested. Because of its potential for runoff, some states have banned phosphorous use except on new lawns or when a soil test indicates a need for it.

Lawn fertilizers are available in several forms. Water-soluble fertilizers are applied as granules and are dissolved by irrigation water. They are easy to apply and are less expensive than controlled-release fertilizers, but they must be applied more frequently. Controlled-release fertilizers release nutrients more slowly, sometimes over a period of years. Organic fertilizers decompose in the soil to release mineral nutrients slowly over a long period of time. Organic materials are more expensive and bulky than manufactured fertilizers, but they can be added less frequently.

In addition, a variety of special lawn fertilizers are available. Winterizer fertilizers are typically high in potassium and, although intended for fall application, can be applied in spring as well. Weed and feed products contain a broadleaf weed killer for weeds, such as dandelions, or a preemergence herbicide to control crabgrass and other annual weeds. Lawn starter products, typically high in phosphorus, are intended for newly seeded lawns.

Depending on your grass type, your climate, the type of fertilizer, and your level of maintenance, fertilizer applications can range from 4 or 5 applications a year to one or even none.

Controlling Thatch

Thatch should be ¾ inch thick or less. Use a dethatcher to reduce thatch levels in the lawn.

Dethatchers have vertical rotating blades that slice through turf, cutting out thatch.

Thatch is the tightly intermingled layer of partially decomposed stems and roots of grass that develops between the actively growing grass and the soil surface. Thatch is normal in a lawn, but when it is thicker than ¾ inch, the lawn begins to suffer. It slows grass growth by restricting the movement of water, air, and nutrients in the soil. As the layer accumulates, the grass roots grow into the thatch instead of down into the soil. This can lead to thinning or even death of grass during summer heat and drought.

Thatch is encouraged by overly vigorous grass growth caused by excessive fertilizing and frequent watering. To determine if your thatch layer is deeper than ¾ inch, cut and lift several plugs of grass 2–3 inches deep.

To reduce thatch and increase the lawn's vigor, power rake or dethatch the lawn. Dethatch cool-season grasses in fall and warm-season grasses in late spring or early summer. Avoid dethatching while new growth is turning green. Dethatchers, also called verticutters, have vertical rotating blades that slice through turf, cutting out thatch. They can be rented, or you can hire a contractor. Mow the lawn as short as possible. Go over it one to three times with the dethatcher. Remove the debris, fertilize, and water to hasten the lawn's recovery.

Compacted Soil

The pressure of foot or vehicle traffic can pack soil tightly, squeezing the pores closed. This restricts root growth and can lead to unhealthy grass plants.

If possible, correct soil compaction before planting by tilling the soil and working in organic matter. In established lawns, relieve compaction by aerating the soil. A soil aerator removes cores of soil and brings them to the soil surface. Aerate when the soil is moist but not muddy. Make passes over the compacted ground in alternate directions until holes are within 3 inches of each other. Leave the cores on the soil or drag a heavy board over them to break them up.

To prevent soil compaction, keep traffic off the soil. Make paths, or place fences or shrubs to act as barriers. If heavy equipment must be driven across the soil, make sure the soil is as dry as possible at the time. If foot traffic can't be kept off, mulch the area with 4 inches of gravel or rocks.

PROBLEMS FROM TREES

When trees and grass grow in the same area, two problems often develop: surface roots, and excess shade from tree canopies and fallen foliage.

The most common cause of surface rooting is lawn watering. Lawn sprinklers tend to water shallowly, causing tree roots to move upward to get moisture. Excess standing water and compacted soil can also cause tree roots to move upward, seeking oxygen.

Alleviate surface rooting by adjusting watering practices and reducing soil compaction around large trees. If this doesn't help, some root pruning may offer a temporary solution. This is best done by a professional. Other possible solutions are placing a ring of bark mulch around the base of the tree or planting a ground cover so you don't have to mow over the tree roots.

To increase the amount of sunlight under trees, try trimming back or cutting off low-growing limbs. Thinning a dense tree crown can also help. If the area receives at least two hours of direct sun daily, a shade-tolerant grass can probably survive. In an area that receives less than 2 hours of direct sunlight each day, consider planting a shade-tolerant nongrass ground cover. Always remove fallen leaves under deciduous trees planted in lawn areas. Fallen foliage shades grass even when light shade is available.

Exposed tree and shrub roots mar the look of a healthy lawn. Prevent their development by improving soil aeration and watering deeply.

Most turfgrasses fail to thrive in shade. Use a shade-tolerant turfgrass variety for areas under trees.

Shady areas call for less fertilization (about ½ as much as turf grown in sun) and greater care in mowing. Letting the shaded grass grow a little taller than the grass in the sun will increase its leaf blade area and result in healthier plants.

Chapter 3

Dealing with Lawn Problems

Examine problem areas close-up and from afar. Determine your level of tolerance before deciding on a treatment for your lawn's problem.

Ortho's *Lawn Problem Solver* is designed to help you diagnose lawn problems and provide potential solutions. The key to accurate diagnosis is knowing how to look for clues to a problem. The checklist on page 13 will help you develop a case history, eliminate unlikely explanations for sources of the problem, and find the real cause.

How to observe

Begin by examining your lawn from a distance. Note its general condition. Is the entire lawn affected or only select areas? Dig up a patch and examine the roots and thatch layer. A 5- to 15- power hand lens allows you to see insects or symptoms

not easily visible to the naked eye. Investigate soil drainage, depth, and type, and test the pH of the soil.

If initial inspection reveals no obvious reason for the symptoms, a case history for the plant may lead you to the cause of the problem.

Putting it all together

Look through the general problem headings at the tops of the pages in the problem-solution section. Find the heading that applies to your problem, then see if one of the descriptions fits your problem. Read carefully. "May" means that the symptom develops only sometimes. Note the time of year to expect the problem

and where to look for the symptoms.

Unfortunately, lawns frequently develop more than one problem at a time. When one problem weakens a plant, other problems are able to infect it.

Once you determine what the problem is, decide on a level of treatment. Not all problems require treatment. Many are purely cosmetic and don't affect the overall health of the plant. Many diseases are most effectively treated with preventative fungicides; if possible, spray before symptoms are seen. Decide what level of injury to your lawn you can tolerate before deciding on a treatment.

If you are unsure of the diagnosis, seek the help of a professional.

CHECKLIST FOR DIAGNOSIS

Use this checklist to develop a case history for the problem and to identify symptoms that will lead to an accurate diagnosis.

WHAT TO LOOK FOR

PLANT CHARACTERISTICS
■ What type of grass is it and when was it established?
■ Does it prefer moist or dry conditions?
■ Can it tolerate cold, or does it grow best in a warm climate?
■ Does it grow best in acid, neutral, or alkaline soil?

LOCATION OF LAWN
■ Is the lawn located near a large body of fresh water or salt water?
■ Is the property located downwind from a factory, or is it in a polluted urban area?
■ Is the property part of a new housing development that was built on a landfill?
■ Is the lawn next to a building? If so, is the location sunny or shady?
■ How close is the lawn to a road? Is salt used to deice the road in the winter?
■ Are there large shade trees overhead?

SYMPTOM DEVELOPMENT
■ When were the symptoms first noticed?
■ Have symptoms been developing for a long time, or did they appear suddenly?

CONDITION OF LAWN
■ Is the entire lawn affected, or is the problem found only on parts of the lawn?
■ What parts of the grass plant show abnormal development?
■ Are the blades atypical in size, color, shape, or texture?
■ What do the roots look like? Are they white and healthy, or are they discolored?
■ Do you see any insects, or is there evidence of insects, such as holes in the blades or chewed roots?
■ Has the problem appeared in past years?

WEATHER AND SUNLIGHT
■ Have weather conditions been unusual (cold, hot, dry, wet, windy, snowy, and so on) recently or during the past few years?
■ How much light does the lawn receive? Is it the optimum amount for this type of turfgrass?

SOIL CONDITIONS
■ What kind of soil is the lawn growing in? Is it predominantly clay, sand, silt, or loam?
■ How deep is the soil? Is a layer of rock or hardpan beneath the topsoil?
■ What is the pH of the soil?
■ Does the soil drain well, or does water remain on the surface after a heavy rain or watering? Does the soil have a sour smell?
■ Is the soil hard and compacted?
■ Was the topsoil removed during construction?
■ Is something buried under the problem spot?

RECENT CARE
■ Has the lawn or surrounding gardens been fertilized or watered recently?
■ If fertilizer was used, was it applied according to label directions?
■ Has the lawn been treated with herbicide, fungicide, or insecticide?
■ Was the treatment for this problem or another one?
■ Was the pesticide registered for use on this type of lawn? (Is this type of grass listed on the product label?)
■ Was the pesticide applied according to label directions?
■ Did rain wash off the spray immediately after it was applied?
■ Did you repeat the spray if the label suggested it?
■ Did you spray on a windy day?

WEEDS

Hand-pulling is easier on the back with long-handled weeders.

In general, lawn weeds are a sign that growing conditions are not optimal for grass. The correct lawn grass for the area, put in properly and given prime care, can usually preclude newly arriving weeds. Weeds thrive in areas where planting practices have been poor, soil unimproved, water minimal, and fertilizer scarce. In the ongoing lawn weed battle, your primary control strategy is to create optimal growth conditions for planted grass that will crowd out weeds.

Weeds are categorized as broadleaf or grassy, annuals or perennials, and as warm-season or cool-season. It is important to properly identify your weeds to properly control them.

Warm-season annuals germinate in late spring and peak at midsummer. The seeds are not shade tolerant, so a thick lawn will deter their presence. Examples include foxtail, goosegrass, and sandbur.

Cool-season annuals generally start growth from seeds in late summer or fall and grow until the first hard frost. They return in spring to set seed before dying out in summer. Examples include shepherd's purse, downy brome, prostrate knotweed, black medic, and common groundsel.

Grasslike perennial weeds are a different color and texture than lawn grasses, ruining the lawn's overall appearance. Examples include dallisgrass, nimblewill, nutsedge, wild garlic and wild onion, crabgrass, and velvetgrass. Bermudagrass and zoysiagrass can become weeds when grown in cool-season lawns.

Perennial broadleaf weeds make a lawn appear ragged. Many of them have flowers that stand out against the green grass. The list includes plantain, chickweed, ground ivy, speedwell, clover, and dandelion.

Effective hand weeders have tines that close around the weeds' roots.

USING CHEMICAL CONTROLS

If you can't control weeds through cultural practices, you may need to resort to chemical control. Herbicides are generally grouped into two categories: preemergent and postemergent. A preemergent stops sprouting at an early stage and is only effective when applied before weed seeds germinate. A postemergent control is effective after the weeds have emerged and begun to grow.

Read the herbicide label carefully before purchasing and using the product. Make sure the chemical is appropriate for the plant you want to treat, and see if using the product requires special precautions. Use all controls at the appropriate time. Avoid spraying or dusting on windy days. Wind can waft weed killers to nearby plants. Apply chemical controls early in the morning or at dusk, when the air is generally calm. If the herbicide label lists a nearby plant as particularly sensitive to the control, protect the plant with a cardboard or wood barrier when you spray.

A treatment can take from 3 to 10 days to produce visible results. Do not reapply the product if weed browning does not occur a day or two after spraying. Herbicide overdoses are dangerous to surrounding grasses. Weed killers do not gain effectiveness if mixed at a concentration stronger than the instructions recommend. Using too strong a mixture

Herbicides require proper timing to be effective. Spot treat individual plants or use a broadcast spray to treat large areas.

A weed-free lawn not only looks nicer, it is also better able to fight disease and insect problems.

can damage or kill nearby desirable plants.

Don't use a weed killer on newly seeded lawns, even if the control is not supposed to affect grass of the type that is planted. Any type of weed control used around seedling grasses can kill them.

Wash all applicators thoroughly with water and detergent to remove traces of herbicides. Better yet, use separate applicators for herbicides, fungicides, and insecticides.

DISEASES

Most lawn diseases are caused by fungi that thrive in cool, moist conditions. They can be spread by wind or splashing water or live in the soil. To reduce chances of infection, do all you can to keep the leaf blades dry. Water in the early morning so plants have time to dry off well before cooler evening temperatures set in. To reduce infection from soilborne diseases, improve drainage and water less frequently so the soil has a chance to dry out between watering cycles.

A healthy lawn is the best defense against disease problems. Choose a grass variety based on your climate and level of maintenance; improve soil conditions if necessary; water, fertilize, and mow appropriately; and maintain a thatch layer of less than ¾ inch.

Most fungicides provide a protective barrier on the leaf blade surface. To be effective, they must be applied before the spore lands on the leaf, so timing is important with fungicidal sprays. The fungicide must also be renewed periodically as it wears off. Once symptoms develop, it's usually too late to spray for the current season. The following year, treat with an appropriate fungicide before symptoms appear. Always read the label carefully before applying any chemical control.

BLUEGRASSES' RESISTANCE TO DISEASES[1]							
Variety	Dollar Spot	Rust	Fusarium Blight	Fusarium Patch	Helminthosporium Leaf Spot	Red Thread	Stripe Smut
A-34		r				r	r
Able I					r	r	
Adelphi	r		r	r	r	r	r
Ascot	r				r	r	
Barcelona				r	r		r
Baron		r			r		
Birka				r	r	r	r
Blacksburg					r	r	r
Bonnieblue	r	r	r	r	r	r	r
Brunswick			s		r		
Eclipse	r				r	r	r
Fylking		r	s				
Glade		r	r		s		r
Majestic	r	r			r		
Merion			s		r	r	
Miracle		r		r	s		
Newport			s				r
Nugget			s		r		
Parade	r		r		r		
Park	r	r	s		s		
Pennstar		r	s		r		
Ram I			s	r	s		r
Rugby		r	r		r		
Sydsport		r			r		r
Touchdown	r			r	r	r	r
Vantage	r	r			r		r

[1] r indicates resistance; s indicates susceptibility

LAWN PESTS

Lawn pests are usually grouped into two categories: insects and larger animals.

Insect pests can invade in small or large numbers. Healthy lawns can tolerate more insect damage than poorly maintained lawns. Large populations of any pest insect species usually call for intervention by the gardener. Predators—such as birds, parasitic wasps, ladybugs, and green lacewing larvae, or pathogens such as *Bacillus thuringiensis* (Bt)—can help control insect pests without chemical application.

Insect pests can either be blade or root feeders. Insecticides are available for both types of feeding. It is important to identify the pest and its damage before deciding on any chemical control. Always read the label carefully before applying any chemical pesticide control.

Moles, rabbits, and gophers top the list of lawn-destroying animals, although in certain areas armadillos, skunks, crayfish, birds, and voles (also called meadow mice or field mice) can cause significant damage. Control methods include trapping, baits, repellents, installation of barriers, and removal of food sources.

Mole tunneling results in irregular ridges in the lawn.

Skunks often tear out large patches of turf looking for insects.

Grub feeding results in large irregular brown patches in late summer.

Chapter 4
Lawn Problems

How to use this book

The photographs at the top of the pages are arranged so that similar symptoms are grouped together. Select the picture that looks most similar to your problem.

The solution section of each problem assumes that you have seen the problem at the time when the symptoms first become obvious. Each solution begins by telling you what you can do immediately to alleviate the problem. Then it tells you what changes you can make in the environment or in your lawn-care practices to prevent the problem from recurring.

When Ortho has products to treat a problem, the products are identified by name. If Ortho does not make a product to solve a particular problem, generic chemical solutions—the common name of the active ingredient—are recommended. When an Ortho product is listed, it will do the job for which it is recommended, and it will not harm your plant if you use it according to label directions. Be sure that the plant you wish to spray is listed on the product label. Always read pesticide labels carefully and follow label directions to the letter.

Group of similar symptoms

A photograph depicting a typical symptom or organism

The problem name

The problem section describes the symptom or symptoms.

The analysis section describes the organisms or cultural conditions causing the problem, including life cycles, natural processes, typical progress of the problem, and its seriousness.

Fusarium patch

Fusarium patch.

Mow grass short in fall to prevent fusarium patch.

A range map of the United States and southern Canada accompanies each problem. In areas that are red, the problem is severe or commonplace. In areas that are yellow, the problem is secondary or occasional. In areas that are white, the problem is rare or nonexistent.

Problem: Yellow-green spots a few inches in diameter form, usually when the snow melts but possibly any time during cool weather from late fall to early spring, even if no snow is present. Spots grow and become pinkish white. Affected leaves become matted and turn light tan while patches grow outward from a rusty pink border. A patch can grow up to 1 foot in diameter. Circular patches can join, displaying extensive damage.

Analysis: A plant disease that primarily affects cold-season grasses, fusarium patch (also known as pink snow mold) is caused by the fungus *Microdochium nivale*. Active only at cold temperatures (32–60°F) when moisture is abundant, fusarium patch is most likely to occur after snow has been on the ground for several months. Prolonged cold weather worsens symptoms; turf quickly recovers if warm weather follows the melting of snow. Prolonged rainy periods in winter also promote this disease. Serious infection leads to crown and root rot.

Solution: Reduce shade in infected areas. Do not apply excessive nitrogen-rich fertilizer in the fall. Overly tall grass is susceptible to fusarium patch, so mow lawns in autumn before snowfall. Reduce thatch buildup. Lightly infected turf usually recovers on its own. For seriously affected areas, apply Scotts® Lawn Fungus Control according to label directions.

The solution section provides short-term and longterm techniques to mitigate or cure the problem.

DEAD OR OFF-COLOR PATCHES, GENERAL
Chemical or fertilizer burn

Burn caused by a fertilizer spill.

An edge guard fertilizer spreader.

Problem: Grass dies and turns yellow in irregular patches or in definite, regular stripes or curves. Grass bordering the areas is a healthy green color. Yellow areas do not spread or enlarge. They appear within 2–5 days after fertilization or after a chemical has been spilled on the lawn.

Analysis: Chemicals such as pesticides, fertilizers, gasoline, and hydrated lime may burn the grass if applied improperly or if accidentally spilled on turf. When excessive amounts of these materials contact grass plants, they cause the blades to desiccate and die.

Solution: Prevent or minimize damage by picking up the spilled material, then washing the chemical from the soil immediately. If the substance is water soluble, water the area thoroughly— 3–5 times longer than usual. If the substance is not soluble in water, such as gasoline or oil, flood the area with a solution of dish soap diluted to about the same strength as used for washing dishes. Then water as indicated above. Some substances, such as herbicides, can't be washed from the soil. In such a case, replace the top foot of soil in the spill area. Prevent further damage by filling gas tanks, spreaders, and sprayers on an unplanted surface, such as a driveway. Apply chemicals according to the label instructions. Apply fertilizers when the grass blades are dry and the soil is moist. Water thoroughly afterward to dilute the fertilizer and wash it into the soil. Keep drop spreaders closed when stopped or turning.

Dog urine injury

Dogs can be lawn pests as well as favored pets.

Close-up of dog urine spots in lawn.

Problem: Circular spots, straw brown in color and 8–10 inches in diameter, appear in the lawn. A ring of deep green grass may surround each patch. Other patches may be dark green in color, without any dead areas in them. No spots or webbing appear on the grass blades, and the grass does not mat. Dogs have been in the area.

Analysis: Dog urine burns grass. The salts in the urine cause varying stages of damage, from slight discoloration to outright death. The nitrogen in the urine may encourage grass immediately surrounding the spot to grow rapidly, resulting in a dark green, vigorous ring of growth. Lawns suffer the most damage in hot, dry weather.

Solution: Water the affected areas thoroughly to wash away the urine. This reduces but does not eradicate the brown discoloration. Surrounding grass eventually fills in the affected areas. For quick repair, spot-sod. If possible, keep dogs off the lawn.

Salt damage

Dead patch from salt accumulation.

Sidewalk deicers may damage turf.

Problem: Grass slowly dies, especially in the lowest areas of the lawn. A white or dark crust may be present on the soil.

Analysis: Salt damage occurs when salt accumulates in the soil to damaging levels. This can happen in either of two ways: (1) the lawn does not receive enough water from rainfall or irrigation to wash the salts from the soil, or (2) the drainage is so poor that water does not pass through the soil. In either case, as water evaporates from the soil and grass blades, salts that were dissolved in the water accumulate near the surface of the soil. In some cases, a white or dark brown crust of salts forms on the soil surface. Salts can originate in the soil, in irrigation water, or in applied fertilizers.

Solution: The only way to eliminate salt problems is to wash the salts through the soil with water. If the damage is only at a low spot in the lawn, fill in the spot to level the lawn. If the entire lawn drains poorly, improve drainage by aerating according to the directions on page 10, or improve the soil as described on page 6. If the soil drains well, increase the amount of water applied at each watering by 50 percent or more, so that excess water will leach salts below the root zone of the grass. Fertilize according to the instructions in the nitrogen deficiency section on page 53.

Seeds fail to grow

Poor seed germination.

Bare spots in newly seeded lawn.

Problem: Seeds in newly planted lawns sprout slowly or not at all, or seedlings rot and fall over at the soil line.

Analysis: Lawn seeds may not grow for several reasons.

1. Lack of water: Once the seed germinates, the soil must stay evenly moist. If the soil around the seedling dries out, the seedling will die; however, excessive water may rot seeds and seedlings.

2. Temperature: Seeds planted at the wrong time of year, when the temperature does not promote healthiest growth, take longer or fail to sprout. If planted at the proper time, seeds should sprout within 4 weeks of planting.

3. Old seeds: Seeds left over from the previous year will sprout if they've been stored in a cool, dry place. Seeds older than one year and seeds that have not been stored properly sprout poorly, if at all.

4. Seeds planted too deep: Seeds planted deeper than ¼–½ inch usually don't sprout.

5. Unprepared soil: Seeds must be in direct contact with the soil to sprout. Seeds that sprout in thatch or directly on top of the soil may dry out.

6. Damping-off: This plant disease is caused by fungi (*Pythium* and *Rhizoctonia*). If the soil is too wet and is rich in nitrogen, damping-off is likely. It kills seedlings either before or after their emergence.

Solution: Solutions below correspond to the numbered items in the analysis above.

1. Water a newly planted lawn frequently enough that only the surface is allowed to dry out. To conserve moisture, mulch the seedbed lightly with a ¼-inch layer of straw or sawdust.

2. Plant warm-season grasses (bermudagrass, centipedegrass, and bahiagrass) in late spring or early summer as the weather warms. Plant cool-season grasses (rye, fescue, bentgrass, and bluegrass) in early to mid-fall or as early as practical in spring.

3. Use seed produced for sale in the current year. Check the seed testing date on the box before purchasing.

4. After sowing the seed, gently rake the soil to mix the seed into the top ¼ inch.

5. To ensure good soil contact, till or rake the soil surface before planting; don't throw seed on top of thatch or unprepared soil.

6. When reseeding blank spots, spray the seedbed with a fungicide containing metalaxyl or captan. Fill in any low spots where water may puddle. Water less often; let the soil surface dry slightly between waterings until seedlings are 1 inch tall.

Sod fails to establish

Dying patches of sod.

Water frequently to keep sod moist.

Problem: Newly sodded areas turn yellow, then brown. Sod rolls up easily like a carpet. No roots are visible on the bottoms of the sod pieces.

Analysis: Sod should establish in 2–3 weeks. Test by gently tugging a corner. If the sod resists tugging, then the roots have grown into the soil. Sod can fail to establish for several reasons.
1. Sod dried out: Sod is susceptible to drying out until its roots grow into the soil.
2. Unprepared soil: If the sod is laid directly on thatch, it dries out quickly. If it is laid on hard soil, the roots have difficulty growing into the soil.

3. Old sod: Old sod has many yellow grass blades among the green blades. It may be weak from water or heat stress and will establish poorly or not at all. Sod may be damaged by remaining rolled for 2 days or fewer in hot weather. In cool weather it can remain rolled for up to a week without damage.
4. Time of year: Sod can be installed almost any time of the year, but it will establish slowly if it is laid when the grass is not actively growing.

Solution: The numbered solutions below correspond to the numbered items in the analysis above. (For information on sod, *see page 7.*)
1. Water frequently enough to keep the sod and the soil under it moist.
2. Before laying sod, till or thoroughly rake the soil. Remove all dead grass and debris, and level the grade.
3. Choose uniformly green sod that is not turning yellow or pale green. Lay the sod as soon as possible. Don't leave it rolled and stacked for more than a day in hot weather. It can be stored rolled for 2–3 days in a shady area, however. Keep the soil on the outer pieces moist.
4. Lay cool-season grass sod (bluegrass, bentgrass, or tall fescue) in late summer, early fall or early spring. Avoid midsummer. Lay bermudagrass, St. Augustinegrass, bahiagrass, or centipedegrass sod in late spring or early summer.

DEAD OR OFF-COLOR PATCHES, DISEASES
Brown patch

Whitish tufts from brown patch.

Characteristic ring around brown patch.

Problem: Circular patches of dead grass a few inches to a few feet in diameter appear in the lawn during periods of high humidity and warm temperatures (75–85°F). Dark purplish smoky rings sometimes surround brown areas. Filmy white to tan tufts may cover grass in the early morning if the dew is heavy. After 2–3 weeks, the center brown grass may recover and turn green, and brown areas form a doughnut shape.

Analysis: Brown patch is caused by a fungus *(Rhizoctonia solani)*. It is one of the most prevalent diseases in warm, humid areas, attacking all types of turfgrass. Lush, tender growth from excessive nitrogen fertilization is the most susceptible to attack. Sometimes only the blades are affected, and the grass recovers in 2–3 weeks. When the infection is severe and warm weather continues, the disease attacks plant crowns and kills the grass.

Solution: Control brown patch with Scotts® Lawn Fungus Control. Apply when the disease is first noticed and at least 3 more times at 14-day intervals. Repeat the treatments as long as warm, humid weather continues. Keep grass as dry as possible to slow down disease spread. Water only in the morning, 1 or 2 times per week. To reduce recurring infections, follow the cultural practices for mowing and watering described on page 8.

Dollar spot

Dollar spot damage.

Close-up of blade damage from dollar spot.

Problem: The grass turns light brown to straw colored in circular areas from the size of a silver dollar to 6 inches in diameter during the warm, wet weather of May to June and September to October. The small dead areas may merge to form large irregular patches. Small, light brown blotches with reddish brown borders appear on the leaf blades. These spots extend across the entire width of the blade. In the early morning before the dew dries, a white cobwebby growth may cover the infected grass blades.

Analysis: Dollar spot, also called small brown patch, is caused by a fungus (*Sclerotinia homoeocarpa*). It is most active during mild (60–80°F), moist days and cool nights. It attacks many kinds of lawn grasses but is most severe on bentgrass, bermudagrass, and Kentucky bluegrass. Lawns troubled by dollar spot are usually under stress from lack of moisture and nitrogen. An infection seldom causes permanent damage, although the lawn takes several weeks or months to recover. Shoes, hoses, mowers, and other equipment spread the fungus organisms.

Solution: Control dollar spot with Scotts® Lawn Fungus Control. Make applications as needed, at 2- to 3-week intervals, beginning when the disease is first evident. The grass recovers quickly if treated promptly. Keep grass as dry as possible. Water only in the morning, 1–2 times per week. It is important to maintain proper nutrient levels; applying nitrogen will help the lawn to recover if it has a nitrogen deficiency.

Fusarium blight

Fusarium blight.

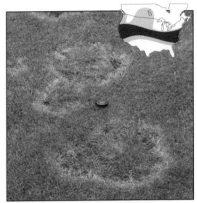

Growth in dead area creates a frog's-eye.

Problem: During hot weather, dead patches form in bluegrass lawns in enlarging rings that may grow up to a foot in diameter. Weeds invade the center of a dead spot, creating a frog's-eye appearance. Patches may merge to form large dead areas. Each patch begins as a circular grayish green area about 2 inches in diameter. The grass in these patches grows slowly, wilts easily, and dies to a yellow-brown color in hot weather. Eventually weeds invade the entire dead circle.

Analysis: Fusarium blight is caused by a soil-borne fungus *(Fusarium)*, often in combination with one or more other pathogenic fungi. It primarily attacks Kentucky bluegrass and annual bluegrass. The disease begins as a small spot, then grows. As it kills the grass, the dead spot fills in with resistant plants, usually weeds, causing the frog's-eye look. This is a hotweather disease that usually develops in hot, dry, windy conditions.

Solution: Once symptoms are well developed, it's too late to treat for the current season. Irrigate regularly to keep the thatch and soil evenly moist. Avoid heavy nitrogen fertilization. The following spring, treat with Scotts® Lawn Fungus Control or a fungicide containing mancozeb or triadimefon before or as soon as symptoms appear. When replanting, select a resistant variety of bluegrass, choose ryegrass or fine fescue, or plant a mix of 20 percent (by weight) perennial ryegrass and 80 percent Kentucky bluegrass, which is more resistant to fusarium blight than pure bluegrass.

Fusarium patch

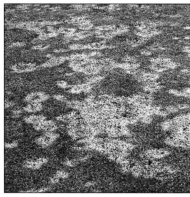

Fusarium patch.

Mow grass short in fall to prevent fusarium patch.

Problem: Yellow-green spots a few inches in diameter form, usually when the snow melts but possibly any time during cool weather from late fall to early spring, even if no snow is present. Spots grow and become pinkish white. Affected leaves become matted and turn light tan while patches grow outward from a rusty pink border. A patch can grow up to 1 foot in diameter. Circular patches can join, displaying extensive damage.

Analysis: A plant disease that primarily affects cold-season grasses, fusarium patch (also known as pink snow mold) is caused by the fungus *Microdochium nivale*. Active only at cold temperatures (32–60°F) when moisture is abundant, fusarium patch is most likely to occur after snow has been on the ground for several months. Prolonged cold weather worsens symptoms; turf quickly recovers if warm weather follows the melting of snow. Prolonged rainy periods in winter also promote this disease. Serious infection leads to crown and root rot.

Solution: Reduce shade in infected areas. Do not apply excessive nitrogen-rich fertilizer in the fall. Overly tall grass is susceptible to fusarium patch, so mow lawns in autumn before snowfall. Reduce thatch buildup. Lightly infected turf usually recovers on its own. For seriously affected areas, apply Scotts® Lawn Fungus Control according to label directions.

Necrotic ring spot

Necrotic ring spot.

Power aerate to reduce compaction and thatch.

Problem: Circular patches of straw-colored or red blades appear. The patches may be from 6 inches to several feet in diameter and usually form a ring around a patch of healthy grass. The result is a doughnut-shape depression. Eventually the dead part of the ring fades to tan. When several patches are present, the area takes on a pockmarked look. Patches spread outward, eventually joining together to form a large blighted area.

Analysis: Caused by the fungus *Leptosphaeria korrae,* this disease occurs from March through November. It appears most frequently in spring and fall when hot, dry conditions follow cool weather. Dense turf with excessive thatch buildup is especially susceptible. Necrotic ring spot is most prevalent in compacted soils and heavily thatched lawns, especially on exposed sites and steep slopes. It can affect most types of lawn grasses, including bermudagrass, Kentucky bluegrass, fescues, ryegrass, and zoysiagrass.

Solution: Dethatching and regular aeration help prevent necrotic ring spot. Avoid drought stress and apply the required amounts of fertilizer. During hot summer months, leave grass a little longer than in cool periods. This helps keep the soil cool, a condition detrimental to the spread of the fungus. Apply Scotts® Lawn Fungus Control or a fungicide containing azoxystrobin or fenarimol. Fertilize regularly with Scotts® Turf Builder® to encourage lawn to fill in. Reseed seriously affected areas.

Pythium blight

Pythium blight on seedlings.

Close-up of white threads of pythium.

Problem: In hot, humid weather from April to October, the grass wilts, shrivels, and turns light brown in irregular spots ½–4 inches in diameter. Spots enlarge rapidly, forming streaks 1 foot wide or wider or patches 1–10 feet in diameter. Infected grass blades mat together when walked on. Blades are often meshed together by white threads in the early morning before the dew dries. Grass sometimes dies within 24 hours.

Analysis: Pythium blight, also called grease spot or cottony blight, is caused by a fungus *(Pythium)*. It attacks lawns under stress from heat (85–95°F), poorly drained soil, and excessive moisture. Dense, lush grass is the most susceptible. All turfgrasses are affected, ryegrasses the most severely. The fungus spores spread easily in free-flowing water, on lawn mower wheels, and on the soles of shoes. The disease is difficult to control because it spreads so rapidly. Pythium blight commonly develops in the fall on top-seeded ryegrass.

Solution: Treat the lawn with a fungicide containing azoxystrobin, metalaxyl, chloroneb, or terrazole as soon as the disease is noticed. Repeat treatments every 5–10 days until either the disease stops or cooler weather resumes. Keep traffic off the diseased area to avoid spreading spores. Don't overwater in hot, humid weather. Severely infected areas often do not recover, so reseed or resod to reestablish the lawn. Treat the new lawn during hot, humid weather. Wait until cool weather to overseed ryegrass.

Spring dead spot

Spring dead spot on bermudagrass.

A healthy stand of bermudagrass.

Problem: Circular dead spots develop in bermudagrass lawns when the lawn begins growth in the spring. Spots vary from a few inches to several feet in diameter. The dead grass is sunken and straw-colored, and the stolons and roots are blackened and decayed. Weeds may invade the affected areas. Bermudagrass sometimes slowly fills in by the end of summer, but the grass is shorter than the surrounding healthy grass. Grass may grow back only in the center of the spot, creating a frog's-eye or island pattern. In bermudagrass lawns that have been overseeded with a cool-season grass, affected areas appear as light green spots.

Analysis: Spring dead spot is caused by fungi (*Leptosphaeria korrae, Ophiosphaerella herpotricha,* and *Gaeumannomyces graminis* var. *graminis*) that affect bermudagrass, causing stolon and root rot. Spring dead spot is common in areas where temperatures drop low enough to promote winter dormancy of bermudagrass. It is most likely to develop in lawns with excess thatch and in lawns that are overfertilized or fertilized late in the growing season.

Solution: Avoid overfertilization and late-season fertilization. Keep thatch to a thickness of no more than ¾ inch. Keep the lawn healthy and vigorous to encourage bermudagrass regrowth into dead areas. Replace the sod and soil of badly diseased areas. Apply a fungicide containing azoxystrobin, myclobutanil, or fenarimol in late summer or early fall.

Summer patch

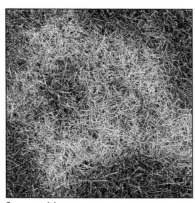

Summer patch.

Determining thatch layer.

Problem: Scattered patches of dead turf 1–2 feet in diameter appear during hot summer weather. Usually the dead grass forms a ring around a patch of healthy grass, creating a frog's-eye pattern. If hot weather persists, the center of the patch also dies. Patches are usually circular or crescent shaped, although serpentine patterns sometimes occur.

Analysis: Summer patch usually occurs from June through September, when hot, dry weather follows a wet period. The disease is caused by a fungus (*Magnaporthe poae*) that infects the roots during cool weather (60–65°F), usually in late spring. When hot weather arrives, the roots can't provide enough water, and the top dies. Summer patch is most prevalent in compacted soils and lawns with excessive thatch buildup, especially on exposed sites and steep slopes. It is worsened by infrequent watering and excessive nitrogen applications. It can affect many types of lawn grasses, including bentgrass, Kentucky and annual bluegrass, and fescue—especially when cultivars are unsuitable for local conditions. The symptoms of necrotic ring spot (*see page 28*) are so similar to those of summer patch that the two diseases can't readily be distinguished outside the lab.

Solution: Dethatching and regular aeration help prevent summer patch, as do frequent, light waterings and regular but light applications of nitrogen. Apply Scotts® Lawn Fungus Control to infected areas. Reseed seriously affected areas with appropriate cultivars.

Armyworms

Armyworm damage to lawn.

Close-up of armyworm larva.

Problem: Armyworms chew grass blades and stems, causing circular bare patches in lawns. In large numbers, armyworms can chew a lawn to the ground in three days. The young worms are up to ¾ inch in length and are usually tan to pale green with faint stripes. The larger, mature worms are 1½–2 inches long, with yellow, orange, or dark brown stripes, and three light hairlines down their backs. The sides have a wider dark stripe and a wide yellow stripe, splotched with red.

Analysis: Armyworms are the larvae of 1-inch-wide tan or mottled gray moths. Like the adults, armyworms are most active at night and on overcast days. In daylight, they hide in the soil around grass roots. The first generation, which appears in spring, causes the most damage. Armyworms are traditionally pests of lawns and turf areas in the Midwest and southern states. However, from time to time conditions are "right" for them to become troublesome in other areas of the country. They get their name from their feeding habits. After they have eaten everything in one area, they crawl in droves to another area in search of more food. Infestations by the thousands can occur on lawns.

Solution: Lawns can be kept alive during moderate infestations with watering and fertilizer. *Bacillus thuringiensis* is partially effective as a natural control of larvae. Homeowners should consider using an insecticide control for armyworms when they notice 4 or 5 small, young, healthy armyworms per square foot of lawn. Use Ortho® Bug-B-Gon MAX® Insect Killer for Lawns. To control armyworms and fertilize your lawn, apply Scotts® Turf Builder® with SummerGuard®. Repeat applications may be needed. Unfortunately, by the time damage is noticed, the armyworms are usually full-grown and insecticides are of little benefit.

Billbugs

Billbug damage.

Billbug larva.

Problem: The grass turns brown and dies in expanding patches from mid-June to late August. When pulled, the grass lifts easily. Lying in the soil are fat, humpbacked white grubs with brown heads and no legs, and from ¼ to ½ inch long. Adults—black, slow-moving, snouted weevils ¼ to ½ inch long—occasionally walk on sidewalks and driveways in May and October.

Analysis: The larvae of billbugs (*Sphenophorus* species) damage lawns by hollowing out the grass stems and chewing off the roots. They can destroy an entire lawn. In May, the adults lay eggs in holes they chew in grass stems. The newly hatched larvae feed inside the stems, hollowing out the stem and crown and leaving fine sandlike excrement. Large larvae feed on roots.

Solution: Control billbugs with Scotts® GrubEx® Season-Long Grub Killer. Repeated treatments are not usually necessary unless the billbugs are migrating from neighboring yards. Small damaged areas usually recover if the larvae are killed. Water and fertilize the lawn to stimulate new growth. Reseed or resod large areas. Maintain proper soil moisture and turfgrass fertility programs.

Black turfgrass ataenius beetle

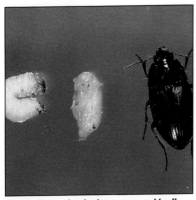

Black turfgrass ataenius larva, pupa, and beetle.

Ataenius beetles attack bluegrass.

Problem: Turf on fairways, tees, and greens (rarely home lawns) wilts despite abundant moisture. Damage begins in late spring and becomes worse with hot, dry weather. Small irregular dead patches converge to form large dead sections. Weakened and dead turf is easily removed, revealing numerous pupae and grubs of various sizes. Grubs are similar to young European chafer and Japanese beetle grubs but are much smaller (⅛–¼ inch long). Adults are reddish brown to shiny black beetles, also ⅛–¼ inch long.

Analysis: The black turfgrass ataenius beetle (*Ataenius spretulus*) prefers closely mowed annual and Kentucky bluegrasses and bentgrasses. Only one generation occurs per year in the North; 2–3 generations occur from the middle latitudes south. Adults overwinter in nearby wooded areas, among leaf litter and mulch, and return to turf in early spring. The grubs cause damage by feeding on roots where soil and thatch meet. Damage is heaviest just before larvae pupate in early summer.

Solution: Control with Scotts® GrubEx® Season-Long Grub Killer as soon as damage is apparent. One application is sufficient. To prevent damage next year, apply GrubEx in late April. Control annual bluegrass weeds to make the lawn less attractive to females.

Chinch bugs

Chinch bug damage.

Close-up of adult chinch bug.

Problem: In April through October the grass wilts, turns yellowish brown, dries out, and dies in sunny areas and along sidewalks and driveways. To check for chinch bugs, select a sunny spot on the edge of an affected area where yellow grass borders healthy green grass. Cut out both ends of a tin can. Push one end of the can 2–3 inches into the soil. Keep it filled with water for 10 minutes. Black to brown insects with white wings ⅛–¼ inch long float to the surface. Pink to brick-red nymphs with a white stripe around the body may also be numerous in the lawn.

Analysis: Chinch bugs (Blissus species) feed on many kinds of lawn grasses, but St. Augustinegrass and zoysiagrass are favorites. Both the adults and the nymphs suck the juices out of the grass blades. At the same time, they inject a poison that causes the blades to turn brown and die. Heavy infestations may completely kill the lawn. These sun- and heat-loving insects seldom attack shady lawns. They can move across an entire lawn in several days.

Solution: Control chinch bugs with Ortho® Bug-B-Gon MAX® Lawn & Garden Insect Killer Ready-to-Spray or Ortho® Bug-B-Gon MAX® Insect Killer for Lawns as soon as you see damage. Mow and water the lawn before spraying, applying ½–1 inch of water to bring the insects to the surface. To prevent recurring damage from newly hatched nymphs, treat every 2 months until frost. In southern Florida, repeat the applications year-round.

Cutworms

Surface cutworm.

Black cutworm damage on golf green.

Problem: Cutworm feeding causes 2-inch-wide bare spots in the lawn. Closer examination shows grass sheared off at or below ground level. Cutworms are brown, gray, or nearly gray; there are spotted and striped varieties. A full-size larva can be up to 2 inches long. Cutworms curl up into a C-shape when touched.

Analysis: The larvae of moths, cutworms feed on grass stems and leaf blades. Adults are dark 2-inch-wide night-flying moths. Often called miller moths, they are common at night around outdoor lights.

Cutworms feed at night. During the day, they hide in the upper soil layers. Some types never emerge, feeding only on grass roots. Birds often seek out cutworms as a source of food.

Solution: *Bacillus thuringiensis* sprays and parasitic wasps help destroy cutworms. Controls include Scotts® GrubEx® Season-Long Grub Killer. It is best when applied before larvae hatch or when they are newly hatched. For proper application in most areas, apply anytime from late spring through midsummer. Ortho® Bug-Geta® Plus Snail, Slug & Insect Killer can also be used. Apply anytime you see signs of listed pests. Repeat treatment every 2 weeks or as needed. During periods of high rainfall or frequent watering, it may be necessary to treat more frequently. Apply chemical controls in late afternoon or early evening for best results.

European crane fly

European crane fly larva.

Adult European crane fly.

Problem: Yellow-brown patches appear in summer during dry seasons. Damage often begins at the lawn periphery and moves inward. The brownish wormlike maggots develop a tough skin and are sometimes called leatherjackets. A larva is about 1 inch long. Secondary damage to the lawn can occur when birds, attracted to larvae, scratch at the surface.

Analysis: Adults look like long-legged mosquitoes. An adult's body size, not including the legs, is about 1 inch long. Crane flies do not sting or do other harm. To determine whether damage is caused by crane fly larvae, water damaged areas thoroughly, then cover them overnight with black plastic. If crane fly larvae are present, they will be lying on the soil surface under the plastic the next morning. Crane fly feeding stops naturally in mid-May. A healthy lawn is usually not seriously damaged by crane fly feeding.

Solution: Treatment is most effective in early April. Dig a patch about 12 inches square and about 2 inches deep. Count the number of larvae in this patch. More than 25 larvae is a sign of trouble. Treatment should consist of an April application of Ortho® Bug-B-Gon MAX® Insect Killer for Lawns to prevent further damage. Severely damaged lawns may need renovation. It is not necessary to treat these lawns with insecticides prior to renovation, as normal site preparation (tilling and renovation) controls larvae. Birds are important predators of crane fly larvae; if insecticides are used, great care should be taken not to poison birds.

Grubs

Grub damage in lawn.

Close-up of grubs.

Problem: From August through October the grass appears to wilt and turns brown in large, irregular patches. Brown areas of grass roll up easily like a carpet. Milky white grubs from ⅛ to 1 inch long, with brown heads and 3 pairs of legs, lie curled in the soil. Birds and animals may be digging in the lawn.

Analysis: Grubs are the larvae of different kinds of beetles, including May and June beetles (also called white grubs) and Asiatic, Japanese, and masked chafer beetles. The grubs feed on turf roots and may kill the entire lawn. Some birds and animals dig up the lawn to feed on the grubs. Adult beetles don't damage the lawn, but they lay eggs in the soil. May and June beetles lay eggs in the spring and summer. Asiatic, Japanese, and masked chafer beetles lay eggs in mid- to late summer. Eggs hatch and grubs feed on roots 1–3 inches deep in the soil. In late fall they move deep into the soil to overwinter; they resume feeding in spring.

Solution: Apply Scotts® GrubEx® Season-Long Grub Killer from late spring to mid- summer to prevent young grubs from damaging your lawn. For best results apply June through July.

Mole crickets

Mole cricket damage.

Mole cricket.

Problem: Small mounds of soil are scattered on the soil surface. The lawn feels spongy underfoot. Large areas of grass turn brown and die. To determine if the lawn is infested with mole crickets, make a solution of one ounce of liquid dishwashing detergent to 2 gallons of water. Drench 4 square feet of turf with the mixture. Mole crickets—greenish-gray to brown insects, 1½ inches long, with shovel-like feet—will come to the surface within 3 minutes.

Analysis: Several species of mole crickets (*Scapteriscus* and *Gryllotalpa* species) attack lawns. They prefer bahiagrass and bermudagrass but also feed on St. Augustinegrass, zoysia, and centipedegrass. They damage lawns by tunneling through the top 1–2 inches of soil, loosening it and uprooting plants so that the plants dry out. Mole crickets also feed on grass roots, weakening the plants. They feed at night and may tunnel as many as 10–20 feet per night. In the daytime, they return to their underground burrows. Adults migrate to new areas twice a year, from March to July and again from November to December.

Solution: In June or July, after the eggs hatch and before the young nymphs cause much damage, treat the lawn with Ortho® Bug-B-Gon MAX® Insect Killer for Lawns. Mole crickets are not active in dry soil, so mow and water thoroughly before applying. If damage continues, treat again in late summer to early fall. Keep the lawn watered to encourage new root growth.

Sod webworms

Sod webworm damage.

Sod webworm.

Problem: From mid-May to October the grass turns brown in patches the size of a saucer in the hottest and driest areas of the lawn. These areas may expand to form large irregular patches. Grass blades are chewed off at the soil level. Silky white tubes are found nestled in the root area. Inside are light brown or gray worms with black spots, from ¼ to ¾ inch long.

Analysis: Several different moths with similar habits are called sod webworms or lawn moths. These night-flying moths drop eggs into the grass as they fly. The eggs hatch into worms that feed on grass blades at night or on cloudy, rainy days. In the daytime the worm hides in white silky tubes in the soil. Sometimes an entire lawn is killed in a few days.

Solution: Control sod webworms with Ortho® Bug-B-Gon MAX® Lawn & Garden Insect Killer Ready-to-Spray, Ortho® Bug-B-Gon MAX® Insect Killer for Lawns, or Scotts® Turf Builder® with SummerGuard® when large numbers of moths are noticed at dusk or at the first sign of damage. First rake out all the dead grass and mow the lawn. Water thoroughly before treating. For best results, apply the insecticide in the late afternoon or evening, when the worms are most active. If using Ortho® Bug-B-Gon MAX® Lawn & Garden Insect Killer Ready-to-Spray, don't cut or water the lawn for 1–3 days afterward. Water Ortho® Bug-B-Gon MAX® Insect Killer for Lawns or Scotts® Turf Builder® with SummerGuard® after spreading. To avoid recurring damage, treat the lawn again every 2 months beginning in late spring or early summer. Damaged lawns may recover rapidly if the insects are controlled early.

Wireworms

Bury potatoes in the lawn to trap wireworms.

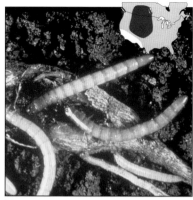

Wireworms have a hard, shiny exoskeleton.

Problem: Irregular areas of wilted grass. Shiny, hard, jointed, yellow to reddish-brown worms are found in the soil.

Analysis: These brown hard-shelled larvae are the offspring of click beetles. The click beetle makes a clicking sound when turning from its back to its feet. The female adult beetles lay their eggs in May and June. After the eggs hatch, the wireworms feed for 2–6 years before maturing into adult beetles. A full-size larva is 1½ inches long.

Wireworms bore into the underground parts of the stem and feed on grass roots. The boring causes the plants to wither and die. They do not feed on above-ground plant parts. They are most prevalent on poorly drained, moist, compacted soil. Wireworms are often found in large groups in an area of the lawn.

Solution: Wireworms can be difficult to control. Create a trap by digging several 3-inch-wide by 3-inch-deep holes in the lawn. Bury a potato in each hole and mark each one by inserting a stake or some other device in the ground. In a few days the potatoes will be filled with feeding wireworms. Remove and destroy the potatoes; do not compost them.

DEAD OR OFF-COLOR PATCHES, WEEDS
Annual bluegrass dying

Annual bluegrass dying.

Annual bluegrass seed heads.

Problem: Areas of grass that were once lush and green die and turn straw brown. Grass appears whitish in late spring, and with the onset of hot summer weather, these places become irregular dead patches.

Analysis: Annual bluegrass (*Poa annua*) is one of the most troublesome but least noticed weeds in the lawn. This member of the bluegrass family is lighter green, has more shallow roots, and is less drought tolerant than Kentucky bluegrass. As its name suggests, annual bluegrass usually lives only for one year, although some strains are perennial. The seed germinates in cool weather from late summer to late fall. Annual bluegrass grows rapidly in the spring, especially if the lawn is fertilized then. Seed heads appear in mid- to late spring at the same height that the grass is cut. The seed heads give the lawn a whitish appearance. When hot, dry weather arrives, the plants turn pale green and die. The seeds fall to the soil and wait for cooler weather to germinate. Annual bluegrass is most serious where the soil is compacted.

Solution: When dead patches appear in hot weather, the annual bluegrass is dead. The lawn is laced with its seeds, however, which will germinate with cooler fall weather. Patch the dead spots. When the weather begins to cool in the fall, treat the lawn with Scotts® Halts® Crabgrass Preventer to kill the seeds as they germinate. Don't cut the lawn too short. Lawns more than 2½ inches tall have very little annual bluegrass. Aerate the lawn in compacted areas *(see page 10)*.

Crabgrass dying

Crabgrass dying.

Spreading plant form of smooth crabgrass.

Problem: Brown patches develop in the lawn with the first fall frost. Close examination of the dead spots reveals a weed instead of lawn grass.

Analysis: Crabgrass (*Digitaria* species) is an annual grassy weed. It forms large, flat clumps, smothering lawn grass as it spreads. Crabgrass dies with the first killing frost in the fall or with the onset of cold weather, leaving dead patches in the lawn. Crabgrass sprouts from seeds in early spring.

Solution: In early spring, two weeks before the last expected frost, treat the lawn with Scotts® Halts® Crabgrass Preventer. This preemergent weed killer kills the seed as it germinates. Kill actively growing crabgrass with Ortho® Weed-B-Gon® Crabgrass Killer for Lawns. Maturing plants are harder to kill. Repeat treatments two more times at 4- to 7-day intervals if necessary. Prevent crabgrass by keeping the lawn at least 2½ inches tall. A deep, thick lawn seldom contains much crabgrass. (For information on crabgrass, *see page 65.*)

Warm-weather grasses become dormant

Dormant bermudagrass is brown.

Bermudagrass stolons creep across the ground.

Problem: Brown patches of irregular shape and size develop with the first fall frost. The leaf and stem structure looks different on the dead grass than on the living grass. No signs of insect or disease damage appear.

Analysis: Warm-weather perennial grasses become dormant with the onset of cold weather. The tops die back, but the perennial roots live over the winter and resprout in the spring. Two of the most common invading warm-weather grasses are zoysiagrass and bermudagrass. They turn brown in the fall, while cool-weather grasses (bluegrass, fescue, and bentgrass) remain green through the winter. (For information on bermudagrass, *see page 64.*)

Solution: Eradicating these grasses from the lawn is very difficult. Once the grass turns brown, it is too late to treat. The following year, spot-treat the undesirable grasses with Ortho® Grass-B-Gon® Garden Grass Killer. If new plants emerge in the spring, spot-treat with the same herbicide. Reseed or resod bare spots.

GRASS THIN
Drought

Lawn damaged by drought.

Tire tracks and footprints show in a droughty lawn.

Problem: Footprints in the lawn make a long-lasting imprint instead of bouncing right back. The grass blades turn a dull bluish-green or slate-gray color and wilt. In the cool evening, the grass recovers until the following day when sun and heat make it darken and wilt again. Areas begin to thin out. After a few days the lawn begins to look and feel like straw and dies.

Analysis: A lawn suffers from drought damage when water evaporates from the lawn faster than the roots absorb it. Drought damage occurs first in the hottest and driest areas of the lawn where sun is reflected—along sidewalks, driveways, south- or west-facing slopes, south sides of buildings, and areas with sandy soil. Grass blades don't wilt as broadleaf plants do. They don't droop but, instead, roll or fold up lengthwise.

Solution: Water the lawn immediately, following the guidelines on page 8. If the grass has turned yellow, the affected areas will require several weeks to recover. If you aren't conscientious about watering, plant a drought-tolerant turfgrass. For information on drought-tolerant grasses, see the chart on page 5.

Leaf spot

Lawn with leaf spot.

Leaf spot on grass blades.

Problem: The grass turns brown to reddish brown and thins out in irregular patches 2 or more feet in diameter from spring until fall. Both the green and the brown grass blades have small oval spots with dark maroon borders and straw-color centers.

Analysis: Several fungi (*Bipolaris*, *Drechslera*, and *Exserohilum* species) can cause leaf spot. Many were formerly called helminthosporium leaf spots. Melting out is common and very destructive to Kentucky bluegrass. In cool spring and fall weather, leaf spot occurs on grass blades but doesn't kill them. In warm summer weather the fungi can kill the grass blades, spread to the base of the plant, and kill entire plants. Lawns that are excessively lush from high nitrogen fertilizing or under stress from short mowing, thick thatch, and frequent watering are the most susceptible to fungal leaf spot attack.

Solution: Spray the lawn with Scotts® Lawn Fungus Control when leaf spotting is first noticed. Make at least 3 more applications, 7–10 days apart. Keep your lawn healthy and vigorous by following the guidelines for lawn care on pages 8–11. Be particularly careful to use a balanced lawn fertilizer, reduce the thatch layer, and water thoroughly and infrequently. To keep the grass dry at night, avoid watering in early evening or late afternoon.

Nematodes

Nematode damage.

Testing soil for nematodes.

Problem: The grass grows slowly, thins out, and turns pale green to yellow. In hot weather the turf may wilt in irregular patterns. Main roots are short with few side roots, or many roots may grow from one point.

Analysis: Nematodes are microscopic worms that live in the soil. They are not related to earthworms. Nematodes feed on grass roots, damaging and stunting them. The damaged roots can't supply sufficient water and nutrients to the grass blades, and the grass is stunted or slowly dies. Nematodes are found throughout the country but are most severe in the South. They prefer moist, sandy loam soils. They can move only a few inches each year on their own, but they may be carried long distances by soil, water, tools, or infested plants. Testing roots and soil is the only positive method for confirming the presence of nematodes. Contact your local county extension office for sampling instructions and addresses of testing laboratories. Soil and root problems such as poor soil structure, drought stress, nutrient deficiency, and root rot also can produce symptoms of decline similar to those caused by nematodes. Eliminate these problems as causes before sending soil and root samples for testing.

Solution: No chemicals available to homeowners kill nematodes in planted soil. Soil fumigation or solarization, however, can be used to control nematodes before a new lawn is planted.

MOUNDS OF SOIL IN LAWN

Ants and fire ants

Ant hill in lawn.

Fire ant mound.

Problem: Mounds or hills of soil occur in the lawn. Each mound has a hole in the center. Ants scurry about.

Analysis: Ants live underground in hot, dry areas of the lawn. They do not feed on grass, but when numerous, they may damage the plants in several ways. The mounds of soil in their hills smother and kill grass plants. As the ants tunnel among grass roots, the soil may dry out, also killing the plants. Ants feed on newly planted grass seeds and sometimes store the seed in their nests. Fire ants have spread across much of the southern United States and continue to advance into new areas. They are tiny—just ¼ inch or less in length—and react angrily when their nest is disturbed. The ant first bites the skin, then inserts its stinger and injects venom. The ant can sting several times in the same area, and many ants may attack at the same time. Reaction to the stings depends on your degree of allergy, but pustules up to ⅛ inch in diameter develop on the skin within 24 hours and can be very painful and sometimes require medical attention. The mounds of fire ants can be a foot high and can seriously damage mowers and tillers.

Solution: Treat anthills with Ortho® Fire Ant Killer Mound Treatment or Ortho® MAX® Fire Ant Killer Broadcast Granules. Repeat the application as new mounds appear and for as long as the ants are active. Once the ants have disappeared, reseed any bare or dead spots. Fire ants can be killed with Ortho® Orthene® Fire Ant Killer. When sprinkled over the mound, it kills fire ants within hours. Entire colonies are destroyed within a week. Use it to control existing mounds in your yard. Follow it with a broadcast treatment of Ortho® MAX® Fire Ant Killer Broadcast Granules over your yard to kill fire ants already there and foraging ants that can enter from other areas. One treatment protects for up to a year. If you follow the Scotts® Annual Lawn Care Program, as an alternative to Ortho® MAX® Fire Ant Killer Broadcast Granules, apply Scotts® Bonus® S MAX™ Southern Weed & Feed and Fire Ant Killer to your lawn. This practice will feed the grass, kill weeds, and control fire ants at the same time. This two-step process (mound treatment and broadcast treatment) is advocated as the best method for controlling fire ants.

Earthworms

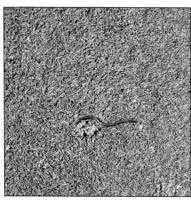

Earthworm on lawn surface.

Close-up of earthworm.

Problem: Small mounds or clumps of granular soil appear scattered throughout the lawn. Earthworms are frequently seen at night or after a heavy rain.

Analysis: Earthworms feed on dead roots and stems and are usually an indication of fertile soil. They prefer moist, medium- to fine-texture soil that is high in organic matter. They are seldom found in dry, sandy soil. Although castings—earthworm excretions that look like small piles of soil—may mar the appearance of the lawn, and earthworms may damage new seedlings, their activity improves the soil in several ways. Their movement from the surface to underlying soil helps mix the organic matter on the top with the soil below and reduces thatch accumulation. Their channels in the soil improve air and water movement through the soil. The castings also help improve the soil structure.

Solution: Earthworms are beneficial to the soil, so control measures are not required. Break up the mounds of soil with a rake or a vertical mower, or treat with a light power rake to even the soil surface.

OFF COLOR, CULTURAL PROBLEMS
Dull lawn mower

Off color caused by dull mower.

Grass blades damaged by dull lawn mower.

Problem: When viewed from a distance, the lawn has a white or gray cast. Leaf ends are ragged and dead at the tips. White hairs may protrude from the cut tips.

Analysis: If a reel or rotary lawn mower is dull, it tears the tips off the grass blades rather than cutting cleanly. This can occur on any grass but especially on perennial ryegrass and tall fescues, which have tough fibers running the length of the blade. If the blade tips are torn, these fibers usually remain protruding from the torn ends. It is particularly important to keep the mower sharp when cutting these grasses.

Solution: Sharpen reel mowers two or three times during the growing season. Sharpen rotary mowers after every few mowings. Reel mowers may be sharpened at a hardware store that offers this service. Rotary mower blades can be removed and sharpened with a file.

Fertilizer

Stripes from uneven fertilizing.

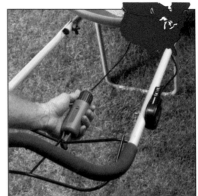

Adjusting the setting on the fertilizer spreader.

Problem: Grass is pale green to yellow or streaked in coloration. Pale areas grow more slowly than others. If the condition persists, the grass becomes sparse and weeds invade.

Analysis: Fertilizers supply the nutrients a lawn needs to grow well and remain healthy. Periodic fertilization is needed throughout the growing season.

Solution: 1. Use a fertilizer that supplies all three major nutrients: nitrogen, phosphate, and potash. For a discussion of plant nutrients, *see page 9*.
2. Too much nitrogen fertilizer during periods of stress promotes lawn diseases. Avoid heavy fertilizing during stress periods. Warm-season grasses are under stress during the cool part of the year; cool-season grasses are under stress during hot weather.
3. Distribute the fertilizer uniformly over the lawn with a properly calibrated drop spreader or a broadcast spreader.
4. Water thoroughly immediately after fertilizer application. This dilutes the dissolved fertilizer and prevents it from burning the lawn.
5. Some general guidelines for feeding grasses: If you live in Zone A or B *(see map on page 5)*, feed in mid-spring, early fall, and late fall. If you live in Zone D or E, fertilize when the grass begins growing in the spring and repeat every six weeks until cool weather. If you live in Zone C and your lawn turns brown every winter, follow the directions for Zone D. If the lawn remains green during the winter, feed in early spring, late spring, early fall, and late fall.

Iron deficiency

Off color from iron deficiency.

Pelletized sulfur for lowering pH.

Problem: Irregular patches of grass are yellow. Individual blades are yellow between the veins; the veins remain green. If the condition persists, the leaves may become almost white and die back from the tips. In severe cases, the grass is stunted.

Analysis: Iron deficiency is a common problem in many plants and is usually caused by alkaline soil conditions. In alkaline soil, much of the iron forms insoluble compounds that are unavailable to grass plants. Lack of iron may also be caused by an iron deficiency, excess phosphorus, a poor root system, overwatering, or the use of water that contains large amounts of bicarbonate salts. Plants use iron in the formation of chlorophyll in the leaves. When iron is lacking, new growth is yellow. Many turfgrass species—including Kentucky bluegrass, perennial ryegrass, fine fescue, creeping bentgrass, and bermudagrass—are susceptible to iron deficiency.

Solution: For a quick green-up, spray the lawn with Scotts® Liquid Turf Builder® Lawn Fertilizer. In the future, fertilize with Scotts® Turf Builder® Lawn Fertilizer with 2% Iron. Lower the alkalinity of the soil by adding ferrous sulfate, ferrous ammonium sulfate, or pelletized sulfur to the lawn. Water the lawn thoroughly after applying one of these amendments. Never add lime to soil in which iron deficiency is a problem. Some turfgrass varieties are resistant to iron deficiency; when replanting, ask for one of these at your garden center or nursery.

Nitrogen deficiency

Unfertilized lawn with green clover.

Fertilizing lawn to increase nitrogen availability.

Problem: Grass is pale green to yellow and grows more slowly than usual. If the condition persists, the grass becomes sparse and weeds invade the lawn.

Analysis: Nitrogen is a key element in maintaining a healthy lawn with few insect and disease problems. Clover stays green because it obtains nitrogen from the air, but grasses can't. It is best to maintain a level of nitrogen in the soil that (1) does not stimulate excessive leaf growth, which would increase the frequency of mowing; (2) does not encourage shoot growth at the expense of root growth; and (3) varies according to the environmental and cultural conditions present. Because heavy rains and watering leach nitrogen from the soil, periodic feedings are necessary throughout the growing season. Acidic soil may cause nitrogen to be unavailable to the grass.

Solution: Apply Scotts® Turf Builder® fertilizer according to the instructions on the label. Properly fertilized lawns are dense and have a nice green color without excessive growth. To prevent burning and to move nutrients into the soil, water thoroughly after application. Grass begins using the nitrogen in the fertilizer within 15–24 hours. Recycle the nitrogen by leaving grass clippings on the lawn if they are not extremely long. If the soil is acidic (below pH 5.5), liming is necessary for effective nitrogen utilization. (For information on soil pH and fertilizing, *see pages 6 and 9.*)

OFF COLOR, DISEASES
Fairy ring

A fairy ring shows up as a large, dark green ring.

Mask fairy ring by applying nitrogen fertilizer.

Problem: Circles or arcs of dark green grass occur in the lawn. The circles may be as small as 1 foot or as large as hundreds of feet in diameter. The grass right inside the darker area may be lighter green than the rest of the lawn. Mushrooms may grow in the dark green area.

Analysis: Fairy ring condition is caused by one of several fungi that grow on organic matter in the soil. The fungus does not harm the grass directly but may inhibit water flow into the soil. The ring of darker green grass is caused by nutrients released as the fungus breaks down organic matter. If the lawn is low in nutrients, the darker area will be more pronounced in contrast to the paler grass around it. The fungus begins growth at a central point and grows outward at a rate of 1–2 feet per year, forming the circle. Mushrooms, which are the fruiting bodies of the fungus, appear when weather conditions are right for them.

Solution: Fairy ring is not a turfgrass disease and does not harm the lawn. It is very difficult to control, but its effects can be masked by fertilizing the lawn outside the ring well and using less fertilizer within the fairy ring so that all the grass will be dark green. If there is a region of pale green or yellow grass within the ring, aerate the lawn and water thoroughly so that water penetrates the soil surface. (For information on aerating, *see page 10*. For information on watering, *see page 8*.) If chemical control is desired, apply a fungicide containing azoxystrobin.

Septoria leaf spot

Septoria leaf spot.

Lawn affected by septoria leaf spot.

Problem: In the spring and fall, the lawn has a gray cast. The tips of the grass blades are pale yellow to gray with red or yellow margins. Pale areas may be ⅛–1 inch long. Tiny black dots are scattered in the diseased spots on blades. From a distance, damage may resemble dull-mower injury.

Analysis: Septoria leaf spot, also called tip burn, is a lawn disease caused by a fungus (*Septoria* species) that infects most northern grass species and bermudagrass. It is most prevalent in the cool, wet weather of early spring and fall. Lawns that have not been fertilized are most susceptible. The disease usually attacks in the spring, declines during the hot summer months, and returns in the fall. Because the disease infects leaf tips first, frequent mowing removes much of the diseased part of the blades.

Solution: Treat the infected lawn with a fungicide containing mancozeb or myclobutanil as soon as discoloration appears. Repeat the treatment 3 more times, 7–10 days apart, or as long as weather favorable to the disease continues. Keep the lawn healthy and vigorous by following the guidelines for good lawn care on pages 8–11. Mow the lawn regularly. Because no variety is completely resistant, plant a blend of 2 or 3 disease-tolerant varieties.

OFF COLOR, INSECTS
Greenbugs

Greenbug damage to lawn.

Greenbugs on turfgrass.

Problem: Areas of discolored grass, ranging from pale green to yellow to burnt orange appear on the lawn, especially in shaded areas. The areas start out small and expand.

Analysis: Greenbugs are small, light green aphids that feed on plant sap. The body is soft, somewhat pear-shaped and narrowed toward the front. When full grown, it is about 1/16 inch long. Greenbugs usually infest Kentucky bluegrass lawns. They feed by inserting their stylet-like mouthparts into the grass blades, sucking out the plant juices, and injecting a toxic salivary secretion that kills cells around the feeding area. Greenbug damage is often noted extending out from the base of shade tree trunks. When greenbug populations are small, symptoms appear as a barely detectable yellowing of the turf. When populations become larger over an extended period, the yellowing becomes much more noticeable, and the grass may even assume a rusty appearance. Continuous feeding can result in the death of infested turf. As the grass is slowly killed, the aphids move as if in a wave from the dead turf area into living grass. They can always be found at the edge of dead areas, moving into healthy grass. It was once thought that the greenbug did not overwinter in the North. However, it isn't unusual for a greenbug population to show up in the same lawn for 2 or more consecutive years. The chance of such a re-infestation by windborne adults seems unlikely. There are several generations per year, and populations can build up very quickly under these conditions.

Solution: A number of insects prey on aphids, including lady beetles, lacewings, big-eyed bugs, ground beetles, syrphid fly larvae, parasitic wasps, and spiders. Heavy populations of these predators and parasites may well be the reason greenbugs are not serious pests in the spring. When greenbug populations explode, predators and parasites cannot suppress the population. Chemical control is often needed where greenbug populations are causing noticeable damage to the turf. Control greenbugs with Ortho® Systemic Insect Killer. If the infestation is in only part of the lawn, spot-treat the infested area. Spot treatments should cover the entire infested area plus a 6-foot band surrounding the infestation. Rainfall during or immediately after a treatment will greatly reduce a spray's effectiveness. Under these conditions, examine the infested area and if greenbugs are seen 24 hours later, repeat the treatment. In addition, do not mow for at least 24 hours after treatment.

Leafhoppers

Leafhopper damage to bluegrass leaf blade.

Close-up of leafhoppers.

Problem: Bleaching or drying out of the grass. Close examination reveals white or yellow patches on green lawn blades. Small insects jump about when you walk through the lawn.

Analysis: Leafhoppers are small, wedge-shape, active insects ⅛–¼ inch long. Adults are whitish-green, yellow, or brownish-gray and may be speckled or mottled. They fly or jump short distances when disturbed. Nymphs are various colors and may have stripes, but no wings. Nymphs have the characteristic habit of moving sideways or backwards when disturbed. Both adults and nymphs suck juices from the leaves and stems of grasses. Adult females insert eggs into tissues of the host plant. Eggs hatch in a few days in warm temperatures. Several generations may occur in a season. With large infestations, leafhopper damage is demonstrated by lawn fading. Severe infestations can eradicate an emerging lawn. Leafhoppers are most abundant in warm weather. The appearance of damaged seedlings may mimic drought injury. However, if leafhoppers are present, they're almost surely doing the damage.

Solution: Small infestations of leafhoppers are usually not bothersome to plants. For severe infestations use Ortho® Bug-B-Gon MAX® Lawn & Garden Insect Killer Ready-to-Spray or Ortho® Systemic Insect Killer.

Mites

Bermudagrass mite damage to lawn.

Close-up of mite damage to bermudagrass.

Problem: Grass turns straw-color, then becomes brown and sparse. Under heavy infestations, a silk-like webbing may be visible.

Analysis: Mites are sucking pests that attach themselves to plant tissue. They suck the sap and cell contents out of leaves. The first sign of damage will show up as small dots on the topside of leaves. Eventually the leaves will turn yellow and fall off. An indication of severe infestation is the presence of webbing. Three types of mites generally infest lawns: bermudagrass mites, which prey on bermudagrass only; clover mites; and winter grain mites, which attack bluegrass, fescue, and bentgrass. Most mites are too small to be seen without a microscope. Under magnification, these $\frac{1}{30}$-inch pests vary in color, depending on the species. They have 8 legs and are insect relatives rather than insects. Bermudagrass mites may be seen by shaking an infested plant over a sheet of dark paper. The mites are visible as creamy specks that begin crawling. Mites thrive in hot, dry weather. Adequate watering keeps populations down. Some gardeners working in areas where mites are present may experience skin irritation from coming into contact with the mites.

Solution: Keep the lawn well watered. Controls include insecticidal soap, Ortho® Bug-B-Gon MAX® Lawn & Garden, and Scotts® GrubEx® Season-Long Grub Killer.

POWDERY MATERIAL ON GRASS
Powdery mildew

Close-up of powdery mildew on grass blades.

Leaf blades infested with powdery mildew.

Problem: Whitish-gray mold develops on the upper surfaces of grass blades during cool, rainy weather. The lawn looks as if it has been dusted with flour. Leaf tissue under the mold turns yellow and then tan or brown. Severely infected plants wither and die.

Analysis: Powdery mildew is a lawn disease caused by a fungus *(Erysiphe graminis)*; it occurs when the nights are cool (65–70°F) and damp, and the days warm and humid. It is most severe on Kentucky bluegrass but also attacks fescues and bermudagrass. Lawns growing in the shade are the most affected. Powdery mildew slows the growth of leaves, roots, and underground stems, causing gradual weakening of the grass and making the grass more susceptible to other problems. Lawns growing rapidly because of excessive nitrogen fertilizing are very susceptible to attack from this fungus. The fine white mildew on the blades develops into powdery spores that spread easily in the wind.

Solution: Treat the lawn with a systemic fungicide when the mildew is first seen. Repeat every 14–28 days as needed. Reduce the shade and improve air circulation by pruning surrounding trees and shrubs. Follow the guidelines on pages 8–11 for a healthy, vigorous lawn.

Rust

Rust on leaf blades.

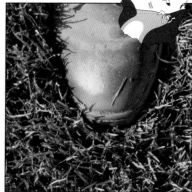

Rust spores on boot.

Problem: Grass turns orange-yellow or reddish brown and begins to thin out. An orange powder that looks like rust coats the grass blades and rubs off on fingers, shoes, and clothing. Reddish-brown lesions under the powder do not rub off.

Analysis: Rust is a lawn disease caused by a fungus *(Puccinia* species) that occurs most frequently on Kentucky bluegrass, ryegrass, tall fescue, and zoysiagrass. It is most active during moist, warm weather (70–75°F) but can be active all winter in mild winter areas. Heavy dew helps its development. Grasses under stress from nitrogen deficiency and lack of moisture are most susceptible to attack. Rust is also more severe in the shade. The orange powder is composed of millions of microscopic spores that spread easily in the wind. Lawns attacked severely by rust are more likely to suffer winter damage.

Solution: Rust develops slowly, often more slowly than the grass grows. Apply a high-nitrogen fertilizer to maintain rapid growth. Mow frequently, removing the clippings. If the disease is severe, treat with a systemic fungicide. Repeat the application every 14–28 days as needed.

Slime mold

Slime mold on leaf blades.

Slime mold on lawn.

Problem: Bluish-gray, black, or yellow pinhead-size balls cover grass blades in the spring, summer, and fall following heavy rains or watering. Balls feel powdery when rubbed between the fingers. Affected areas range in size from a few inches to several feet in width.

Analysis: Slime molds are fungi that feed on decaying organic matter in the soil. They don't feed on green plants. When the powdery covering is heavy, it may damage the grass by shading the blades from sunlight, causing them to turn yellow. Slime molds occur on dichondra, all turfgrasses, and some weeds. While slime molds are feeding on decaying organic matter in the soil, they are white, gray, or yellow slimy masses on the soil. When they are ready to reproduce, they extend up onto grass blades and form powdery balls containing spores. This phase of the life cycle is more noticeable than the slimy mass phase.

Solution: In most cases control is not necessary. Although slime molds are unsightly, they do not permanently damage the lawn. Remove the molds from the grass by spraying with a strong stream of water or by sweeping with a broom.

GRASSLIKE WEEDS
Annual bluegrass

Annual bluegrass seed heads.

Patch of annual bluegrass.

Problem: In mid-spring, abundant seed heads give the grass a whitish appearance. Pale green grassy weeds grow among desirable grasses. They turn yellow and die with the onset of hot weather.

Analysis: Annual bluegrass (*Poa annua*) is one of the most troublesome but least noticed weeds in the lawn. This member of the bluegrass family is lighter green, more shallowly rooted, and less drought tolerant than Kentucky bluegrass. As its name suggests, annual bluegrass usually lives for only one year, although some strains are perennial. The seed germinates in cool weather from late summer to late fall and grows rapidly in the spring. Whitish seed heads appear in mid- to late spring at the same height that the grass is cut. When hot, dry weather arrives, the plants turn pale green and die. The seeds fall to the soil and wait for cooler weather to germinate. Annual bluegrass is most serious where the soil is compacted or overwatered and where drainage is poor.

Solution: Weed killers are only partially effective in controlling annual bluegrass. Prevent seeds from germinating by applying Scotts® Halts® Crabgrass Preventer as a preemergent treatment in late summer to early fall. Don't use if you plan to reseed the lawn in the fall. Replace the dead areas in the summer with sod. Do not cut the lawn too short. Lawns more than 2½ inches tall have very little annual bluegrass. Aerate the lawn in compacted areas (*see page 10*). Space waterings far enough apart that the surface of the ground has time to dry.

Barnyardgrass

Barnyardgrass.

Seed head of barnyardgrass.

Problem: In summer and fall, a low-growing grassy weed with reddish-purple stems 1–3 feet long grows in the lawn.

The smooth leaves of barnyardgrass are ¼–½ inch wide, with a prominent midrib.

Analysis: Barnyardgrass (*Echinochloa crus-galli*), also called watergrass, is a warm-season annual weed that is usually found in poorly managed lawns of low fertility. It reproduces by seeds and develops into a plant with a shallow root system. Although the natural growth habit of barnyardgrass is upright, when mowed regularly it forms ground-hugging mats.

Solution: Kill mats of actively growing barnyardgrass with Ortho® Weed-B-Gon® Crabgrass Killer for Lawns. Improve soil fertility and maintain a dense, healthy lawn by following the guidelines on pages 8–11.

To kill barnyardgrass seedlings as they sprout, apply Scotts® Halts® Crabgrass Preventer in the early spring, 2 weeks before the last expected frost.

Bermudagrass

Bermudagrass stolons creeping over soil.

Bermudagrass seed heads.

Problem: In southern areas of the United States, patches of fine- to coarse-texture grass grows in the lawn. The slightly hairy gray-green stems, or stolons, creep along the soil surface and are 6–18 inches long. Leaf blades are ⅛–¼ inch wide. This grass turns brown in the winter if subjected to temperatures below 40°F.

Analysis: Bermudagrass *(Cynodon dactylon)* is one of the most widely used lawn grasses in the South. It has a very deep root system and is drought and heat tolerant. The leaves are not cold tolerant and turn brown when the temperature approaches freezing. Its vigorous, creeping growth habit makes it a weed that invades other types of lawns and flower beds.

Solution: Spot-treat the bermudagrass with Ortho® Grass-B-Gon® Garden Grass Killer anytime the grass is actively growing, up to 2–4 weeks before the first killing frost. After one week, mow the treated grass as close as possible, and reseed. The grass will still be green when it is mowed, but roots will die in 3–4 weeks and will not resprout. If regrowth occurs in the spring, spot-treat with the same herbicide. This herbicide will also kill any desirable grasses it contacts. To prevent bermudagrass from invading your lawn from other lawns, mow higher than 1½ inches, spot-treat as needed each summer, and water the lawn adequately during the summer. Avoid spreading creeping stems to new areas with lawn mowers. Fertilize more heavily in the fall than at any other time of year if you have a cool-season grass.

Crabgrass

Crabgrass seed head.

Smooth crabgrass.

Problem: A grassy weed forms broad, flat clumps in thin areas of the lawn. It grows rapidly through the summer, rooting at the stem joints. The pale green blades of crabgrass are 2–5 inches long and ⅓ inch wide. Seed heads 2–6 inches tall grow from the center of the plant.

Analysis: Crabgrass (*Digitaria* species) sprouts from seeds in the early spring, growing rapidly and producing seeds all summer until the first killing frost in the fall. Then the plants turn brown and die. The seeds lie dormant over the winter and sprout in the spring. Crabgrass is one of the most common lawn weeds in its area of adaptation. When a lawn begins to thin out from insects, disease, or poor maintenance, crabgrass is one of the first weeds to invade the area.

Solution: Kill actively growing crabgrass with Ortho® Weed-B-Gon® Crabgrass Killer for Lawns. Older plants are harder to kill; repeat the treatment two more times at 4–7-day intervals. To kill crabgrass seeds as they germinate, apply Scotts® Halts® Crabgrass Preventer in late winter or early spring, 2 weeks before the last expected frost (about the time forsythia and dogwood bloom). Follow the guidelines on pages 8–11 for a healthy, vigorous lawn; crabgrass is not usually a serious problem in lawns with thick, healthy growth.

Dallisgrass

Dallisgrass.

Dallisgrass seed head.

Problem: Clumpy rosettes of a coarse-texture grassy weed appear in the lawn. Plants may turn brown in the center.

Analysis: The coarse leaves of dallisgrass *(Paspalum dilatatum),* a perennial grass, are ½ inch wide and 4–10 inches long. Stems 2–6 inches long radiate from the center of the plant in a starlike pattern. Plants grow in spreading clumps with deep roots. Seeds are produced on 3–5 fingerlike segments that grow from the top of the stems from May to October. Silken hairs cover the seeds, which lie dormant over the winter and sprout very early in the spring.

Dallisgrass also reproduces by underground stems. Although it is primarily a summer weed in cool areas, it grows all year in mild climates. Growth begins quite early in spring. Dallisgrass grows best in warm weather; low, wet ground; and high-cut lawns. Once established, however, it spreads rapidly in low-cut lawns. It prefers moist soil but will tolerate any type of soil. It remains green in the winter and is a severe problem in the southern United States.

Solution: Treat actively growing clumps of dallisgrass with Ortho® Weed-B-Gon® Crabgrass Killer for Lawns, Ortho® Grass-B-Gon® Grass Killer, or Roundup® Weed & Grass Killer in early spring or summer. These herbicides will also kill any desirable grasses they contact. Repeated treatments are often necessary, since dallisgrass has deep roots. There is no preemergent control. Try draining soil to eliminate dallisgrass.

Foxtail

Foxtail unmowed plant form.

Foxtail plant form in lawn.

Problem: A grassy weed with a medium green color and coarse texture forms broad, flat clumps in thin areas of the lawn, ruining the overall appearance.

Analysis: Foxtail (*Setaria* species), sometimes called bristlegrass or pigeongrass, is a summer annual that grows 1–2 feet tall. In a mowed lawn, it will form a low mat. The leaves are flat, sometimes twisted, ¼–½ inch wide and 2–6 inches long. Spikelets consisting of 5–20 bristles, 2–4 inches long, appear from July to September. The bristle resembles a fox's tail, hence the name. The bristles contain seeds that sprout from mid-spring to early summer. Annual foxtail grows in clumps and is often mistaken for crabgrass, but it forms smaller clumps than crabgrass. (For information on crabgrass, *see page 65*). Foxtail is found in yards with rich soil bordering fields, roadways, and other unmaintained areas.

Solution: Spot-treat existing weeds in lawns with Ortho® Weed-B-Gon® Crabgrass Killer for Lawns or Roundup® Weed & Grass Killer. These herbicidee will also kill any desirable grasses they contact. Prevent seeds from germinating by applying Scotts® Halts® Crabgrass Preventer in early spring, 2 weeks before the last expected frost (about the same time the forsythia blooms). Since foxtail reproduces only from seeds, rather than from reproducing stems or runners, it can be removed with a trowel or by hand. Keep it under control by removing lawn clippings that contain seed heads.

Goosegrass

Smooth, flat stems of goosegrass.

Goosegrass seed head.

Problem: A grassy weed forms in areas of the lawn. It resembles crabgrass but is darker green with a silver center. Its smooth, flat stems form a rosette that resembles the spokes of a wheel. Leaf blades are 2–10 inches long and about ¼ inch wide.

Analysis: Goosegrass (*Eleusine indica*), also called silver crabgrass and yardgrass, is a warm-season annual. Seeds germinate when soil temperatures are between 60–65°F, several weeks after crabgrass sprouts. It multiplies from seeds, expands by spreading, and has an extensive root system. It doesn't root at stem joints. Seeds are produced on stalks 2–6 inches high that appear from July to October. Mature plants die with the first frost. Seeds are dormant over winter and sprout in spring. Goosegrass has an extensive root system. It prefers compacted soils that have poor drainage and light, frequent watering.

Solution: Treat actively growing goosegrass plants with Ortho® Grass-B-Gon® Garden Grass Killer. This herbicide will also kill any desirable grasses it contacts. Prevent seeds from germinating by using Scotts® Halts® Crabgrass Preventer or a preemergent herbicide containing trifluralin in early spring before plants sprout. Goosegrass is not usually a serious problem in lawns with thick, healthy growth. Reduce soil compaction *(see page 10)* and improve turfgrass growth to compete with amd prevent development of goosegrass.

Nimblewill

Nimblewill.

Brown nimblewill patches in lawn after frost.

Problem: Brown patches appear in the lawn in early spring and do not start to green up until after the third or fourth mowing. A grassy weed with a different texture than the lawn ruins the overall appearance of the lawn.

Analysis: Nimblewill *(Muhlenbergia schreberi)*, also called nimbleweed and dropseed, has smooth, flat, light green or bluish-green leaves up to 2 inches long on wiry stems up to 10 inches tall. The stems grow outward first and then upward from the central crown (where the stem meets the roots). In spring nimblewill turns green after other grasses. Nimblewill stems root at lower nodes as the plant spreads outward. It thrives in hot, dry, gravelly areas and in thin turf during drought. Seeds are produced on inconspicuous spikes from August to October. The seeds lie dormant in the soil for the winter and sprout in late spring. Plants develop a shallow root system. Plant tops turn whitish tan and become dormant with the first killing frost in the fall. They begin growth again late the following spring.

Solution: For small nimblewill infestations dig out patches of the weed. Spot treat it in lawns with Ortho® Grass-B-Gon® Grass Killer or Roundup® Weed & Grass Killer. These herbicides will also kill any desirable grasses they contact. Begin control in early spring. Nimblewill is easiest to kill when it is a seedling, from late spring to early summer. Maintaining a dense, healthy lawn through proper turf selection, establishment, and maintenance is the recommended nonchemical control for nimblewill. Nimblewill is often a problem where commonly grown turfgrasses are poorly adapted. Modifying the growing conditions by improving soil drainage, reducing shade, and increasing air movement may favor turf growth and increase its ability to compete with nimblewill.

Nutsedge

Shiny triangular stems of nutsedge.

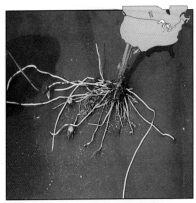

Underground stems and tubers of nutsedge.

Problem: In the summer, this weed grows more rapidly than the grass and stands above the turf. The erect, single, triangular stem has narrow, grasslike, yellow-green leaves arranged in threes from the base of the plant. Seed heads are yellow-brown.

Analysis: Nutsedge *(Cyperus* species), also called nutgrass, is a hard-to-kill perennial weed. Both yellow and purple nutsedge are common weeds. Nutsedge reproduces by underground stems, seeds, and tubers. The tubers, the size of popcorn kernels, sprout in late spring and early summer. Plant tops die back in fall, leaving new tubers in the soil to repeat the cycle the following year. The tubers and underground stems are firmly anchored in the ground. When a plant is pulled up, some of the tubers and underground stems are left behind to resprout into new plants.

Solution: Nutsedge is difficult to control. Treat with Ortho® Weed-B-Gon® Crabgrass Killer for Lawns when the plants first become active in the spring. Repeat 2 or 3 more times 10–14 days apart. If you miss a treatment, the weeds recover and take longer to control. Treat again the following spring to kill any persistent nutsedge tubers. These herbicides may temporarily (for 2–4 weeks) discolor desirable grasses. On centipedegrass and St. Augustinegrass lawns, use Scotts® Bonus® S Weed and Feed in January, February, or March, before the weeds germinate.

Quackgrass

Quackgrass spreads by rhizomes.

Clasping auricles ("claws") of quackgrass.

Problem: A grassy weed with hollow stems grows in a newly seeded lawn. Wheatlike spikes grow at the tips of the stems. The narrow leaf blades are bluish green and rough on the upper surface. A pair of "claws" occurs at the junction of the blade and the stem. Rings of root hairs grow every $\frac{3}{4}$–1 inch along the underground stems.

Analysis: Quackgrass (*Elytrigia repens*), a cool-season perennial, also called couchgrass or witchgrass, spreads extensively through the lawn by long, white underground stems. It reproduces by seeds and these underground stems. The seeds may lie dormant in the soil for up to 2 years. Quackgrass is found most frequently in fertile, newly seeded lawns. It grows much more rapidly than grass seedlings, often crowding them out.

Solution: Quackgrass is difficult to control in lawns. If the entire lawn is infested with it, the lawn will need to be killed and another planted. If only isolated areas are infested, kill them and replant these spots. The quackgrass must be actively growing before it is sprayed. Let it grow to 4–6 inches high, then spray with Ortho® Grass-B-Gon® Garden Grass Killer. This type of herbicide will also kill any desirable grasses it contacts. If regrowth occurs, repeat the treatment.

Tall fescue

Tall fescue in lawn.

Tall fescue as lawn weed.

Problem: Clumps of very coarse, tough grass invade thin areas of the lawn. The medium-dark green blades, each ½ inch wide, are ribbed on the top surface and smooth on the bottom. In the spring and fall, the lower parts of the stems turn reddish purple. The blades tend to shred when mowed.

Analysis: Tall fescue *(Festuca arundinacea),* a cool-season, perennial, bunch-type grass, is very durable. It is commonly used on athletic fields because it holds up well under hard wear. Tall fescue makes an attractive turf when grown by itself. When it is seeded with, or invades, bluegrass, bermudagrass, or ryegrass lawns, however, it is considered a weed. It becomes very clumpy and makes an uneven turf. When insects and diseases attack the desirable grasses in the lawn, the tall fescue is usually not affected. It resists diseases and grubs, and sod webworms attack it only if they've eaten everything else. Tall fescue is also somewhat heat tolerant, and its deep roots help it survive periods of heavy moisture and drought.

Solution: Kill clumps of tall fescue with Ortho® Grass-B-Gon® Garden Grass Killer while it is actively growing from early summer to early fall. Omit a regular mowing before treating to allow for enough leaf tissue to absorb the chemical. This type of herbicide will also kill any desirable grasses it contacts. One week after spraying, mow the tall fescue and reseed the area.

Velvetgrass

Velvetgrass as lawn weed.

Velvetgrass in lawn.

Problem: A weed with bright green velvety leaves that stay flat to the ground appears in the lawn, ruining the lawn's appearance.

Analysis: Velvetgrass (*Holcus mollis*) is a perennial grassy weed. In lawns, plants lay flat and root wherever stem joints touch the soil. The 4- to 8-inch leaves are velvety and bright green. Seed heads 2–4 inches long appear from July to August. Seeds remain dormant over winter and germinate in spring. Plants grow from vigorous, slender underground rhizomes. Velvetgrass thrives in damp areas with good soil, but it tolerates partial shade. It can grow to 4 feet tall in unmowed areas.

Solution: Grassy perennial weeds like velvetgrass are difficult to control. No chemical will kill them without harming your lawn. Spot treat with Roundup® Weed & Grass Killer Ready-to-Use at any time, but spraying before seed heads mature will be most effective. This is a nonselective herbicide that kills all plants it touches, including desirable lawn grass plants. Spray on a calm day and protect nearby desirable plants. Remove the dead grass, prepare the soil, and reseed within 1–2 weeks.

Zoysiagrass

Close-up of zoysiagrass.

Zoysiagrass as a weed in lawn.

Problem: Small to large irregular patches of brown form in spring, fall, and winter, amid cool-season grasses that stay green.

Analysis: Zoysiagrass *(Zoysia japonica)* is a valued lawn grass in warm-weather areas, but can become a grassy weed in other regions. In cold areas, this perennial grass goes dormant with the first fall frosts and remains so until late spring. The result is irregular patches of brown in cool-season lawns such as bluegrass, fescue, and bentgrass. The brown pattern is often attributed to insect invasion, but the zoysiagrass is perfectly healthy though dormant. Its tops have died back, but its roots are merely resting. Though it grows slowly in cool-season areas, zoysiagrass is hardy to Zone 4. It often establishes in heavy traffic areas of the lawn, and then invades surrounding areas.

Solution: Grassy perennial weeds such as zoysiagrass are difficult to control. Mechanical control consists of digging up clumps and reseeding. If zoysiagrass is a continuing problem, some gardeners let it take over lawns growing in full sun, then spray it with green dye in winter. No chemical will kill zoysiagrass clumps without harming your lawn. Spray with Roundup® Weed & Grass Killer Ready-to-Use. This is a nonselective herbicide that kills all plants it touches, including desirable lawn grass plants. Spray on a calm day and protect nearby desirable plants. Remove the dead grass, prepare the soil, and reseed within 1–2 weeks. Chemical treatment should be done while zoysiagrass is still green; once it turns brown, anything but digging is ineffective.

BROADLEAF WEEDS
Black medic

Black medic in flower.

Close-up of black medic flowers and leaves.

Problem: Thick mats of a weed resembling clover appear in the lawn, crowding out desirable lawn grasses. Small, bright-yellow flowers bloom on this weed in late spring and early summer.

Analysis: Black medic (*Medicago lupulina*) is normally a summer annual, but can act as a perennial in some conditions. Other names for black medic include yellow trefoils and black clover. It has a tap root and spreads low to the ground, but it does not root from nodes on the stems. Black medic is more active in soils low in nitrogen fertility. Black medic is shallow rooted with multibranched slender, prostrate, slightly hairy stems spreading 12–24 inches. The alternately arranged, dark green leaves are compound with 3 oval leaflets that are slightly toothed at the tips. The center leaflet is stalked and the side leaflets occur close to the stem. Leaves are sparsely hairy and the leaflets ⅕–⅗ inch long. The ⅛–⅙-inch-long bright-yellow flowers are clustered on short stems that emerge from the leaf axils. Each cluster is approximately ½ inch long, round, and comprised of up to 50 individual flowers. Flowering occurs April to October, but sometimes as late as December in warm-weather areas. Blooms are followed by black kidney-shape seed pods. Black medic is often confused with white clover and yellow woodsorrel.

Solution: Black medic becomes prevalent in nitrogen-deficient lawns. Good turf management practices, including a regular balanced fertilization program, encourages a dense stand of turf and makes it difficult for black medic to persist. Treat the lawn with Scotts® Turf Builder® with Plus 2® Weed Control. If cultural recommendations are insufficient for a previously infested area, apply a postemergence broadleaf herbicide such as Ortho® Weed-B-Gon MAX® during periods of active growth from late spring through early summer and again from early through mid-autumn. Black medic can be hand-pulled.

Clover

Clover in flower.

Patches of clover in lawn.

Problem: A weed with leaves composed of three round leaflets at the top of a hairy leafstalk, 2–4 inches tall, grows in the lawn. The leafstalks sprout from the base of the plant. White or pink-tinged flowers, ½ inch in size, bloom from June to September. They often attract bees.

Analysis: Clover *(Trifolium* spp.) is a common perennial weed in lawns throughout the United States. Although some people like it in a lawn, others consider it messy, or they don't like the bees attracted to the flowers. Clover reproduces by seeds and aboveground rooting stems. The seeds can live in the soil for 20 years or more. The plant, which has a creeping, prostrate habit, suffocates lawn grasses, resulting in large patches of clover. When buying a box of grass seed, be sure to read the label carefully. Clover seeds are sometimes contained in seed mixtures. Because clover produces its own nitrogen, it thrives in lawns that are underfertilized.

Solution: Treat the lawn with Ortho® Weed-B-Gon MAX®, Ortho® Weed-B-Gon® Chickweed, Clover & Oxalis Killer for Lawns, or Scotts® Turf Builder® with Plus 2® Weed Control in the spring and early fall. Repeated treatments are often necessary for adequate control.

Common chickweed

Common chickweed.

Common chickweed stem tips and flowers.

Problem: A weed with small (½-inch-long) teardrop-shape leaves and starlike white flowers grows in thin spaces in the lawn. A single row of white hairs appears on one side of the stem. The stems root easily at their joints. Common chickweed is most often found in shady or moist areas.

Analysis: Common chickweed (*Stellaria media*) grows from seeds that sprout in the fall; the plants live for less than a year. Common chickweed grows primarily in damp, shady areas under trees and shrubs and on the north side of buildings, but it can also occur in dormant warm-season grasses. Common chickweed invades home lawns when they begin to thin out from insects, disease, mechanical damage, or shade. It reproduces by seeds and by the creeping stems that root at their joints wherever they touch the soil. It has a low, prostrate growing habit, forming a dense mat that crowds out the grass.

Solution: Treat the lawn with Ortho® Weed-B-Gon MAX® or Ortho® Weed-B-Gon® Chickweed, Clover & Oxalis Killer for Lawns when chickweed is growing actively in the early spring or late fall. Repeated applications may be necessary. Do not water for 2 days after applying.

Dandelion

Close-up of dandelion in bloom.

Lawn infested with dandelions.

Problem: From spring to fall, a weed with bright yellow flowers blooms in the lawn. In southern states it may bloom all winter. Flower stems grow 2–10 inches above the plants. The medium-green leaves, 3–10 inches long, are deeply lobed along the sides. The plant has a deep, fleshy taproot.

Analysis: Dandelion *(Taraxacum officinale)* is the most common and easily identified perennial weed in the United States. It reproduces by seeds and from shoots that grow from the fleshy taproot. This taproot grows 2–3 feet deep into the soil, surviving even the severest of winters. They are most numerous in full sunlight. In the early spring, new sprouts emerge from the taproot. As the yellow flowers mature and ripen, they form white "puff balls" containing seeds. The wind carries the seeds for miles to other lawns. The tops die back in late fall, and the taproot overwinters to start the cycle again in the spring. Dandelions prefer wet soil and are often a sign of overwatering.

Solution: Treat the lawn with Ortho® Weed-B-Gon MAX® or Scotts® Turf Builder® Plus 2® Weed Control. For best results, make two applications, first in the early summer and again in the early fall. Do not water or mow for 2 days afterward. Feed the grass adequately to keep it dense. Mow frequently enough to keep the flowers from becoming seed heads. Hand-digging and removal requires persistence, because pieces of root broken off and left in the soil will sprout into new plants.

Field bindweed

Field bindweed pink flower form.

White form of field bindweed.

Problem: A plant with long twining stems grows across the lawn. The leaves are arrowhead shape and up to 2 inches long.

White to pink funnel-shape flowers, 1 inch across, appear from spring to fall.

Analysis: Field bindweed (*Convolvulus arvensis*), a deep-rooted perennial weed also known as wild morning glory, is found throughout most of the United States in lawns, gardens, and fields and along roadways. It is one of the most troublesome and difficult weeds to eliminate because of its extensive root system. The roots may grow 15–20 feet deep. Roots or pieces of roots left behind from hand-pulling or spading easily resprout. Field bindweed, which reproduces by seeds and roots, twines and climbs over shrubs and fences and up into trees. It prefers rich, sandy, or gravelly soil but will grow in almost any garden soil.

Solution: Treat plants from late spring through early summer or from early to late fall with Ortho® Weed-B-Gon MAX®.

Because of the deep roots, repeated treatments may be necessary. Treat again whenever new growth appears.

Ground ivy

Ground ivy growing in the shade.

Ground ivy in flower.

Problem: A low-growing, creeping weed with rounded, scalloped leaves grows in shady areas of the lawn. The nickel- to quarter-size leaves grow at the end of a long leafstalk. The stalks are paired opposite each other along the square (4-sided) stem. Light blue to purple flowers, ½–¾ inch long, bloom from April to July.

Analysis: Ground ivy (*Glechoma hederacea*), also called creeping ivy or creeping Charlie, is a perennial that was originally planted in some areas as a ground cover. It has now become a major weed in the North. Ground ivy reproduces by seeds and creeping stems that root wherever they touch the soil. This plant has shallow roots and forms a dense mat throughout the lawn, crowding out grasses. Although it is found primarily in shaded areas, ground ivy also survives and spreads in sunlight.

Solution: Treat the lawn with Ortho® Weed-B-Gon MAX® or Ortho® Weed-B-Gon® Chickweed, Clover & Oxalis Killer for Lawns in the spring or fall when the plants are growing actively. Spring treatment gives the best result by killing the plants before the leaves mature. Where the ground ivy has formed a dense mat, it may be necessary to apply the herbicide for several years in a row. Hand-pulling is not a good way to control ground ivy because the roots readily resprout into new plants. Ground ivy may indicate that the area is too shady for a lawn to grow.

Henbit

Patch of henbit in bloom.

Close-up of purple flowers of henbit.

Problem: A weed with rounded, toothed leaves, ¾ inch wide, grows in the lawn. The lower leaves are attached to the square (4-sided) upright stems by short leafstalks; upper leaves attach directly to the stems. Stems root easily at lower joints. Lavender, ½-inch flowers appear from March to June and again in September.

Analysis: Henbit (*Lamium amplexicaule*), a weed also known as dead nettle or bee nettle, is found in lawns and flower and vegetable gardens across the country. It is a winter annual that sprouts from seeds in late summer and grows rapidly in the fall and the following spring, producing conspicuous purple flowers early in the spring. Henbit also reproduces by stems that root easily wherever the stem joints touch the soil. Henbit most frequently invades thin areas in lawns with rich soil.

Solution: Treat the lawn with Scotts® Turf Builder® with Plus 2® Weed Control or Ortho® Weed-B-Gon MAX® in early spring when henbit is growing most rapidly. Do not water for 24 hours after treating. An infestation of a few small plants can be hand-pulled.

Mallow

Leaves and plant form of mallow.

Mallow in bloom.

Problem: A weed with hairy stems, 4–12 inches long, spreads over the lawn. The stem tips turn upward. Round, heart-shape, hairy leaves ½–3 inches wide and slightly lobed along the edges are attached to the stems by a long leafstalk. White to lilac flowers, 2½ inches in diameter with 5 petals, bloom singly or in clusters at the leaf and stem junction. Mallow is often mistaken for ground ivy, but the spreading branches do not root when they contact soil.

Analysis: Mallow (*Malva* species), also called cheeseweed, is found throughout North America in lawns, fields, and along roadways. It is an annual or sometimes a biennial and reproduces by seeds. It has a straight, nearly white taproot that is difficult to pull from the soil. Mallow is most commonly found in poorly managed lawns and in soils high in manure content.

Solution: Treat the lawn with Ortho® Weed-B-Gon MAX® or Scotts® Turf Builder® with Plus 2® Weed Control from midspring to early summer. Maintain a thick, healthy lawn by following the guidelines on pages 8–11.

Oxalis

Close-up of oxalis in bloom.

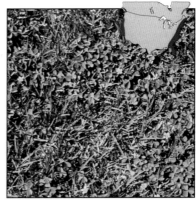

Oxalis in lawn.

Problem: A weed with pale green leaves divided into 3 heart-shape leaflets invades thin areas of the lawn. The leaves are ¼–¾ inch wide and similar to clover. The stems root at the lower joints and are often thinly covered with fine hairs. Small, bright yellow flowers are ½ inch long with 5 petals. Cucumber-shape, light green seedpods develop from the fading flowers. Plants may be 4–12 inches high with a prostrate-to-erect growth habit.

Analysis: Oxalis (*Oxalis stricta* and *O. corniculata*), also called yellow woodsorrel or creeping woodsorrel, is a perennial plant that thrives in dry, open places but may also be a problem in moist, well-fertilized lawns. It often invades lawns that are beginning to thin from insect, disease, or maintenance problems. Oxalis reproduces from the seeds formed in the seedpods. When the pods dry, a light touch causes them to explode, shooting seeds several feet in all directions. Oxalis leaves contain oxalic acid, which makes them sour.

Solution: Control oxalis with Ortho® Weed-B-Gon MAX® or Ortho® Weed-B-Gon® Chickweed, Clover & Oxalis Killer for Lawns. The most effective time to spray is when the weeds are actively growing, in the spring or late summer to fall. Oxalis is not easy to kill; several treatments are usually needed. Check the soil pH level *(see page 6)*, and follow the guidelines on pages 8–11 for a healthy, vigorous lawn. A healthy lawn helps smother the oxalis.

Plantain

Buckthorn plantain in flower.

Broadleaf plantain.

Problem: A weed forming a rosette with long, narrow, hairy leaves 4–12 inches long and held off the ground grows in the lawn. The leaves have 3–5 nearly parallel, prominent veins. Erect white flower spikes, 4–12 inches tall, appear from spring into fall. A similar weed has broad, egg-shape leaves attached to 1-inch leafstalks that are, in turn, attached to the center of a rosette. These leaves are 2–10 inches long, with 5–7 prominent veins, and lie flat on the soil. Erect greenish-white flower spikes, 2–10 inches tall, bloom from spring to fall.

Analysis: Both buckhorn plantain *(Plantago lanceolata)*, with long, narrow leaves, and broadleaf plantain *(P. major)*, with egg-shape leaves, are common perennial weeds that resprout from their roots each year. They reproduce from seeds formed on the flower spikes and from new shoots from the roots. As thin areas develop in the lawn from insect, disease, or maintenance problems, either or both of these weeds can move in. As the plants grow larger and lie flat on the soil, they crowd out the surrounding grass.

Solution: Spray the lawn with Ortho® Weed-B-Gon MAX® in the spring or fall when the plants are actively growing. Repeated applications are often necessary. An application in early fall gives the best results by reducing infestation the following year. Do not mow 5 days before or 2 days after spraying.

Prostrate knotweed

Creeping stems of prostrate knotweed.

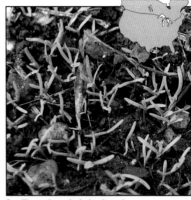
Seedlings of prostrate knotweed.

Problem: A low-growing broadleaf weed forms mats up to 2 feet wide in areas of the lawn. It is especially prevalent in areas with compact, infertile soil such as walkways and recreation areas where the soil and grass are trampled.

Analysis: Prostrate knotweed (*Polygonum aviculare*) is an annual also called knotgrass or doorweed. It grows quite low to the ground and has smooth blue-green oval leaves, each about 1 inch long and ⅛ inch wide. The leaves attach to wiry stems at visible joints. The stems range from 4–24 inches long. Knotweed is an annual that forms mats that can reach 2 feet wide, crowding out lawn grasses. The weed is usually found in compacted soil. The fastest growth period for prostrate knotweed is from early spring to early fall. Tiny green-white flowers bloom in clusters at the leaf and stem joints from June to November. Knotweed reproduces from seeds, which are plentiful. They remain dormant over the winter and germinate in the spring as the soil warms. Though knotweed can't get started in hearty, dense turf, it is common in areas of heavy foot traffic.

Solution: Soil aeration helps control prostrate knotweed. Pull out young plants. There is no preemergent control. If necessary, treat the lawn with Ortho® Weed-B-Gon MAX® or Scotts® Turf Builder® with Plus 2® Weed Control in early spring.

Purslane

Purslane plant form.

Individual purslane stem.

Problem: A low-growing weed with reddish-brown, thick, succulent stems is found in thin areas or newly seeded lawns. The leaves are thick, fleshy, and spoon-shaped. Small yellow flowers sometimes bloom in the leaf and stem joints. Stems root where they touch the soil.

Analysis: Purslane *(Portulaca oleracea),* a summer annual weed that thrives in hot, dry weather, is seldom found in the spring when the lawn is being treated for other weeds. Purslane grows vigorously, forming a thick mat. The small yellow flowers open only in the full sunlight. Purslane primarily invades bare spots in lawns or thin lawns that have not been watered properly. Purslane stores water in its thick, fleshy stems and leaves and therefore survives longer than grass during dry weather.

Solution: Spray the lawn with Ortho® Weed-B-Gon MAX® when the weed is actively growing. If the lawn has just been reseeded, do not treat until the seedlings have grown enough to require mowing 3 times. Wait 3–4 weeks before seeding bare areas. Remove stem pieces from the area to prevent them from rerooting into the soil.

Sheep sorrel

Sheep sorrel foliage and plant form.

Sheep sorrel seed heads.

Problem: Arrow-shaped leaves, 1–3 inches long, with two lobes at the base of each leaf, form a dense rosette. Erect, upright stems grow 4–14 inches tall. Two types of flowers appear in mid-spring; one is reddish green, the other yellowish green.

Analysis: Sheep sorrel (*Rumex acetosella*), a cool-season perennial, is also called red sorrel or sourgrass because of its sour taste and reddish coloration. It grows in dry, sterile, sandy, or gravelly soil and is usually an indication of acidic soil or low nitrogen fertility. Sheep sorrel reproduces by seeds and red, underground root stalks. The root system is shallow but extensive and is not easily removed.

Solution: In spring or fall, treat with Ortho® Weed-B-Gon MAX®. Do not mow for 5 days before or 2 days after treating. Sheep sorrel is difficult to control, so several treatments may be necessary. To discourage sheep sorrel, test the soil pH and correct to between 6.0 and 7.0 if necessary. Improve the soil fertility by following the fertilizing guidelines on page 9.

Shepherd's purse

Shepherd's purse rosette plant form.

Shepherd's purse flowers and seedpods.

Problem: A broadleaf rosette-type weed appears in sunny areas of the lawn. Left unmowed, it grows upright with arrow-shape leaves and white flowers.

Analysis: Shepherd's purse *(Capsella bursa-pastoris)* is also called lady's purse and shepherd's bag. It is an annual that may appear throughout the year in warm-winter areas. Its arrow-shape leaves are toothed or lobed and form a rosette at the base of the plant. Tiny white flower clusters appear on stems that can reach up to 18 inches high. Seeds are in triangular pods resembling small purses. Fall frost kills this annual in cold-climate areas, but seeds can remain dormant for several years before germinating in spring. In warm-weather areas, seeds may germinate in fall. The plants then grow through the winter until fall.

Solution: Shepherd's purse is not fussy about soil, but it will not grow in shade. Control in lawns by hand-pulling. Frequent mowing helps prevent seed formation on this upright plant. Improving soil fertility encourages vigorous, dense grass growth that helps prevent shepherd's purse from becoming established. However, shepherd's purse cannot be eliminated by frequent mowing alone. Once the seeds have germinated, shepherd's purse will thrive at even the lowest mowing height, due to its flat rosette of foliage. Chemical control consists of treatment with Ortho® Weed-B-Gon MAX®. Treat when plants are actively growing. The herbicide is most effective when temperatures are between 60–80°F. Do not spray if temperatures are projected to exceed 85°F within the next 48 hours. Choose a time when no rain is forecast for at least 24 and preferably 48 hours. To avoid herbicide drift, spray only when the air is still. Drift can harm or kill nearby desirable broadleaf plants such as flowers, vegetables, trees and shrubs.

Speedwell

Speedwell in flower.

Foliage of speedwell.

Problem: A creeping broadleaf weed with white or purple flowers forms patches, especially in acidic soil in moist shady areas of the lawn.

Analysis: Speedwell (*Veronica filiformis*), also called creeping veronica, can cover an entire lawn in a few years if left to grow. It has bright green, roundish, scallop-edged leaves ¼ inch long. Each plant is about 4 inches high. Tiny bluish-white flowers bloom on stalks that grow somewhat above the leaves. Seeds are produced in heart-shape pods. The seeds seldom mature, so the plant doesn't reproduce from them. The creeping stems, however, root easily where the stem joints touch the soil. Pieces of stem cut and distributed by lawn mowers also root to start new plants. It is not usually found in well-drained, sunny areas that receive fertilizer regularly. It grows best in moist, shady lawn and acidic soil, but it can grow in sunlight if soil remains moist. There are both perennial and annual varieties of creeping veronica.

Solution: Speedwell is difficult to control. Discourage it by cutting grass short and removing all clippings to avoid stem rooting. Spray with Ortho® Weed-B-Gon MAX® when the plant is flowering or actively growing. When hand-pulling, remove all plant parts from the lawn to discourage rerooting.

Spotted spurge

Close-up of spotted spurge.

Growth habit of spotted spurge.

Problem: A low-growing weed with pale to dark green, oval leaves ¼–¾ inch long appears in the lawn. Each leaf may have a purple spot in its center. Stems ooze milky white sap when broken. The leaves are slightly hairy on the underside and smooth on top. Tiny pinkish-white flowers bloom in midsummer. The many pale green stems fan out on the soil surface and over the top of the grass, forming mats up to 2 feet in diameter.

Analysis: Spotted spurge *(Euphorbia maculata),* also called milk purslane or prostrate spurge, invades thin areas of the lawn, smothering the grass. Spurge sprouts from seeds in the spring and dies with the first frost. This weed commonly invades lawns that are dry and infertile, but it can also be found in well-maintained lawns.

Solution: In the late spring or early summer, treat the lawn with Scotts® Turf Builder® with Plus 2® Weed Control or Ortho® Weed-B-Gon MAX®. Keep the lawn well watered *(see page 8)* to discourage spurge from invading dry areas.

MISCELLANEOUS
Algae

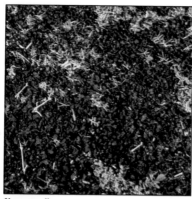

Algae growth.

Core aeration improves drainage of wet soils.

Problem: A green to black slimy scum covers bare soil and crowns of grass plants. When dry, it becomes crusty, cracks, and peels easily.

Analysis: Algae *(Symploca* and *Oscillatoria species)* are freshwater plants that invade shady, wet areas of the lawn. They injure grass by smothering or shading it as they grow over the crowns of the plants. Invaded areas become slippery. Algae live in compacted soil and soil that is high in nitrogen and organic matter. They need constantly or frequently wet conditions to survive. Organic fertilizers encourage algae, especially in the cool seasons. Algae may be carried from place to place by animals, equipment, people, and birds. Water taken from ponds, lakes, and streams and used for irrigation usually contains algae.

Solution: Patches of algae may be sprayed with a fungicide containing mancozeb or wettable sulfur 2 times, 1 month apart, in early spring. This is only a temporary solution. Algae will soon return if the conditions are not corrected. Reduce soil compaction *(see page 10)*. Improve drainage through soil amendment *(see page 6)*, and prune nearby trees to reduce shading. Avoid high-nitrogen fertilizers in late fall and winter. Maintain a healthy, vigorous lawn according to the lawn maintenance guidelines on pages 8–11.

Moss

Moss in lawn.

Close-up of spore heads of moss.

Problem: Green, velvety, low-growing plants cover bare soil in moist, shady areas or in compacted sections of the lawn with low pH.

Analysis: Moss invades thin or bare areas of the lawn. It does not grow in a vigorous lawn. Moss is encouraged by poor fertility, poor drainage, compacted soil, shade, and high acidity. Moss plants sprout from spores and fill in bare or thin areas.

Solution: Shortly after mowing, apply Scotts® Moss Control Granules while grass is moist. Moss may also be removed by hand or power raking. Reduce shade by pruning nearby trees. Correct soil compaction *(see page 10)*, and improve drainage through soil amendment *(see page 6)*. Test the soil pH, and correct it if necessary. Follow the lawn maintenance guidelines on pages 8–11 to promote a healthy, vigorous lawn.

Mushrooms

Mushrooms in lawn.

Toadstools in lawn.

Problem: Mushrooms sprout up in the lawn after wet weather. They may be growing in circles of dark green grass. When the weather gets colder or the soil dries out, they disappear.

Analysis: Mushrooms, also called toadstools or puffballs, live on organic matter buried in the soil. The mushroom is the aboveground fruiting or reproductive structure of a fungus that lives on and helps to decay the organic matter. The organic matter may include buried logs, lumber, roots, or stumps. Most mushrooms do not damage the lawn but are objectionable because they are unsightly. Mushrooms growing in circles of dark green grass, called fairy rings *(see page 54)*, may make the soil impervious to water and injure the grass.

Solution: There is no practical or permanent way to eliminate mushrooms. When buried wood or organic matter is completely decayed, the mushrooms will disappear. The easiest and most practical solution, although it is only temporary, is to break the mushrooms with a rake or lawn mower.

INDEX

METRIC CONVERSIONS

U.S. Units to Metric Equivalents			Metric Units to U.S. Equivalents		
To Convert	**Multiply By**	**To Get**	**To Convert**	**Multiply By**	**To Get**
Inches	25.4	Millimeters	Millimeters	0.0394	Inches
Inches	2.54	Centimeters	Centimeters	0.3937	Inches
Feet	30.48	Centimeters	Centimeters	0.0328	Feet
Feet	0.3048	Meters	Meters	3.2808	Feet
Yards	0.9144	Meters	Meters	1.0936	Yards

To convert from degrees Fahrenheit (F) to degrees Celsius (C), first subtract 32, then multiply by 5/9.

To convert from degrees Celsius to degrees Fahrenheit, multiply by 9/5, then add 32.

Take Them Outdoors!

WATERPROOF BOOKS™

New For Spring 2007
- Scotts Sprinklers and Watering Systems
- Miracle-Gro Container Gardens
- Ortho Lawn Problem Solver

Other Great Waterproof Titles
- Scotts Lawns
- Miracle-Gro Water Gardens
- Miracle-Gro Vegetables
- Miracle-Gro Roses
- Miracle-Gro Perennials
- Ortho Flower Problem Solver

All Your Garden Tools Should Be This Rugged.

Pocket-Size • Cleanable • Durable • Tear-Resistant • Lightweight